LYRICS TO AMUSE

VOLUME I

GRAHAM EARNSHAW

Lyrics to Amuse Volume 1

By Graham Earnshaw

ISBN-13: 978-988-8843-45-9

© 2024 Graham Earnshaw

MUSIC / Lyrics

EB208

All rights reserved. No part of this book may be reproduced in material form, by any means, whether graphic, electronic, mechanical or other, including photocopying or information storage, in whole or in part. May not be used to prepare other publications without written permission from the publisher except in the case of brief quotations embodied in critical articles or reviews. For information contact info@earnshawbooks.com

Published in Hong Kong by Earnshaw Books Ltd.

Foreword

I have been writing songs for five decades, it has long been my main creativity activity. That and performing the songs live in bars. It's a magical and mind-expanding experience. I have written and processed millions of words in other contexts, mostly business articles and books, but the concentrated nature of song lyrics—encompassing an idea and its extensions in a few words and a short few minutes—is special. It is different from prose writing, it is closer perhaps to the use of language in an effective business plan PPT. No words wasted. It's not as fast as a photograph, but it beats the hell out of a book. And how does it compare to a poem? A poem takes as long to absorb as a song, but does not provide the emotional context of the accompanying music.

    Are my songs any good? I think so, otherwise I wouldn't put them out there, but I possess everything but objectivity. What do other people think of them? Part of me yearns to have my songs recognized so I can become a star I tell you, a star (see the lyrics to "Me and the Multitudes"), but another part of me doesn't really care at all. The process of producing a song, the composing of lyrics and then interweaving them with melody and chords, is joyful enough by itself because something always happens which is unexpected. The applause after I finish playing one of them, however, is welcome. There's no money in it, that's for sure, unless you're Ed Sheeran or Billie Eilish. As I say in one lyric, songs are a dime a dozen and hits are a dollar 35. The chorus of that song delves deeper into the issue of my motivation for songwriting: Is it for attention? (no) / Or communication? (no) / A stab at immortality? / Exercise the fingers? / Training for the brain? / No, writing songs is simply better than watching TV.

How do these lyrics and the songs in which they are embedded stack up against the works of other singer-songwriters? It's a subjective call. I am definitely not as good as my heroes, who include for generational reasons, Sting, James Taylor, Tom Waits, Donald Fagan and Paul Simon. But there are a few phrases here and there, and the occasional idea, which I think could rank with the best.

Why publish these lyrics as a book? Firstly because I can. Secondly because almost all these tunes are available on Spotify, Apple Music, Netease Music and many other platforms, but not with the lyrics linked to them, and perhaps listeners would like to be able to read along to the tune. And thirdly perhaps because just reading the lyrics alone could amuse.

The structure of these lyrics is mostly standard – verse and chorus and bridge somewhere in the middle to change the mood and perspective somewhat before returning the sledgehammer of the chorus to reiterate the point. I am pretty radical on perfect rhymes and abhor the laziness of imperfect rhymes so often found in pop music today. Young people, what can you say…

As to lyrical content, most of these songs in some way or another reflect my life, some incident, some element of it. I have included a few comments on some of the lyrics where appropriate to provide context. I have occasionally tried writing songs from other people's perspectives, but they usually don't work. "Household Wares" may be a successful exception. But largely

reflective as they are of my life, I should provide some information for those who do not know me. I was born in England, spent my teens in Australia, moved to Hong Kong at the age of twenty and became fascinated by China and words and popular music. I have been a journalist and a businessman, a teacher and a musician, a writer and a publisher. I have walked across China, I ran the best rock band in China, I have made and lost money. All of it is reflected somewhere in the lyrics I have written.

I agree with Frank Zappa's assessment many years ago that there are already enough love songs out there, and I generally strive to find a way to write songs about other topics. But there are a few love songs here too. One of my abiding goals with most of my songs, and also in conversation, is to try to raise a smile. To amuse.

I have ordered the lyrics here alphabetically, except for two long poems inspired by Stanley Holloway's Albert and the Lion, which are placed at the end. The reason for that approach is that I am incapable of ordering them according to quality, and re-arranging them in some thematic way (China songs, song-writing songs, love songs), would remove the element of the unexpected. I also present them mostly without much indication as to when they were written. Some date from the 1970s, and from every decade after that through to the current 2020s, but I don't think the date is particularly relevant. The songs either work or they don't, regardless of era. The exceptions are songs which are specific to an event, such as "Gorby is a CIA Spy" and "Hong Kong Blues", obviously written before Gorbachev threw in the towel in 1991 and Hong Kong was handed over to Beijing in 1997.

Oh, and "Governor's Blues", written soon after a near mutiny by the Hong Kong police in 1977. Writing songs about current events in a way that is timeless is a trick I haven't learned well.

I still write songs and I have a bunch that are waiting to be finished. Hence the title of this volume. And if you play guitar or another musical instrument and would like to try playing these songs, you can either work them out from the recordings online, or wait for the accompanying book to this one, which will contain chord charts. But first, here are the lyrics.

Table of Contents

1. A Man of No Importance — 1
2. A Cuppa Tea — 2
3. A Dolphin's Plea — 3
4. A Winter's Day — 5
5. AI Is not My Passion — 6
6. All I Can Think Of — 8
7. Always A Way — 10
8. Another Little Drink — 11
9. Armageddon — 13
10. As Old As You Feel — 14
11. Bang Bang Bang — 16
12. Better Than — 18
13. Bird in a Cage — 20
14. Chocolate Fix — 22
15. Come September — 24
16. Concrete Beams — 26
17. Copyright (Is For The Living) — 27
18. Coco Loco — 28
19. Cricket in a Basket — 30
20. Critique — 32
21. Dirty Old Man — 34
22. Elephants — 35
23. Elizabeth — 37
24. Emphasis — 39
25. Everybody has a Price — 41
26. Failure — 42
27. Finish the Rice — 44
28. Flying — 46
29. Fool I Was — 47
30. Front Page Lead — 48
31. Getaways — 50
32. Go Now — 51
33. Good Better Best — 52
34. Good Night — 53
35. Gorby Is A CIA Spy — 54
36. Governor's Blues — 56
37. Green So Green — 58
38. He Who Dies with Most Toys Wins — 59
39. Highway 318 — 61
40. Hong Kong Blues (10,000 conmen) — 62
41. Household Wares — 63
42. How Should I Say It — 65
43. I Care — 66
44. I Like The Rain — 68
45. I'm Me — 69
46. I'm Just Saying — 70
47. It Doesn't Get Better — 71
48. It's Fake — 72
49. It's Good To See You — 74
50. Karma — 75
51. Lady Road — 76
52. Lanterns — 77

53.	Leaving Home Today	79	82.	Status Quo	125
54.	Let's Samba	81	83.	Stomach Acid	126
55.	Life and Death	82	84.	Sunshine	127
56.	Man's Best Friend	84	85.	Take Nothing	128
57.	Mary Corrigan	86	86.	Tao Party	130
58.	Me and the Multitudes	88	87.	The Alien	132
59.	Mid-Life Crisis	89	88.	Talkin' Hong Kong	133
60.	My Own Two Feet	91	89.	That's My Number	135
61.	Never More Thank Now	93	90.	The Beans	136
62.	No Regrets	95	91.	The Deal Is On	138
63.	Nothing Is Allowed	97	92.	The Last Panda	139
64.	Number One	98	93.	The Memory Stays	141
65.	Oh Hugo	99	94.	The Motive	143
66.	One False Move	100	95.	The PCH (Pacific Coast Highway)	145
67.	One Little Million	101	96.	The Priorities	147
68.	One More Day	103	97.	The Road Is Hard	149
69.	Out of the Blue	104	98.	The Sky	150
70.	Out on the Road	106	99.	Time to Rhyme	152
71.	Over the Ridge	107	100.	Tough World	154
72.	Panic Early	109	101.	Trying to Write A Song	155
73.	Peking All-Stars	111	102.	Waiting	157
74.	Racing	113	103.	Was What It Was	158
75.	Real City Heroes	115	104.	Walking West	159
76.	Really Really Really	117	105.	We're All the Same	160
77.	Respect (It Is What It Is)	118	106.	What Lockdown?	161
78.	Room With A View	120	107.	Works of Art	162
79.	Sake O Sake	121	108.	Yoghurt and Honey	163
80.	Satellite	123	109.	Harold, the Kamikaze Strawberry	164
81.	Socialism	124	110.	Agnes & Edwina	167

A MAN OF NO IMPORTANCE

I am just a man of no importance
I will leave no mark on history
Another face in the crowd
Barely worth a glance
There is no magic here,
There is no mystery

    It's a small walk-on role in a play
    But you know I'm sincere
    When I say it's an honor
    That I'm so proud to be here.

What I leave behind is next to nothing
A few words, a few songs, nothing more
But I still win if I can say that what I bring
Leaves the world no worse off
Than it was before.

This play was in progress
Long before we were born
Will continue
Long after we're gone
Mine's a small walk-on role in the play
But you know I'm sincere
When I say it's an honor
Yes I'm so proud to be here.

No matter how dimly my star
Might have shone
I still wonder
Around whom
The world will turn
When I am gone.

I am just a man of no importance
I will leave no mark on history.

A CUPPA TEA

I wrote this song as a jingle and offered it the British Tea Board. They rejected it.

A lump or two of sugar
A little drop of milk
Stir it all together
Tastes as smooth as silk.

   There's nothing like a cuppa tea
   When you're lonely or you're all at sea
   Life isn't such a tragedy
   Just make yourself a cuppa tea.

They say that it's addictive
I don't like that idea at all
If they keep on raising prices,
I'll have to go through withdrawal.

   There's nothing like a cuppa tea
   To build up your energy
   Ask your doctor what's the remedy
   He'll tell you it's a cuppa tea.

Indian or Ceylonese,
Or good old Chinese char
One thing about a cuppa tea,
You always know where you are.

If you're suffering from poverty,
Refugee or amputee
Don't wait around for charity,
Just make yourself a cuppa tea.

   There's nothing like a cuppa tea,
   To banish the monotony
   Pretend you've won the lottery,
   Go on -- have another cuppa tea.

A DOLPHIN'S PLEA

This song was inspired by a novel written by my friend and mentor Andrew Nibley, which takes the view, and who knows maybe it is true, that we are each twinned with a dolphin which follows and shares our inner lives, guiding and comforting us, if we wish to accept their help.

The air is clean
Fuel for destiny's machine
I break the surface,
Breathe and glide
Back down to depths unseen.

To float, to drift away
That's the way to spend a day,
One with oneness,
Timeless, warm
I navigate the way.

Who is this man
The one whose life I steer
The one, whose dreams
For me are so clear

I accept my role
I do not mean to hide
But why him now,
Oh please allow me first,

To reach the other ...
The other side

What is the plan
I'll do all I can

For Love and Understanding
The universe expanding
My questions notwithstanding
I've always tried.

This man's in pain
Here he's struggling again
Caught twixt fantasy and fact
He's verging on insane

If only he could see
What Is clear to me
I will send him dreams of light
And hope they set him free.

Who is this man
The one filled with dismay
The one I try to comfort night and day
All I know
Is that four words guide the flow
Tolerance, kindness, patience, love
As was true for always
From long ago.

What is the plan
I'll do all I can

For Love and Understanding
The universe expanding
My questions notwithstanding
I will strive as long as I'm alive

For Love and Understanding
The universe expanding
My questions notwithstanding
I'm hoping
Today is the day.

A WINTER'S DAY

A love song in 6/8 time

I remember a winter's day,
A long long time ago
The wind was cold, the sky was grey
The city laid out below
I was breathing the scent of her hair
Looking so hard, but trying not to stare

On that winter's day
She was heading home
What on earth could I say
She in colour, me in monochrome
To me she was perfect,
With beauty and style
She looked over at me, and gave me a smile

   And the angels sang
   And the trumpets played
   And the fireworks lit up the sky
   For a moment it seemed
   Like the world was mine
   For a moment it seemed
   As if I couldn't die.

On that winter's day,
A long, long time ago
We walked along, my brain felt like clay
Discussed the weather,
Looked down at the glow
Twisted inside,
I took a second to pray
Then I asked her to go to a movie,
And she said ...
okay.

   And the angels sang
   And the trumpets played
   And the fireworks lit up the sky
   For a moment it seemed
   like the world was mine
   For a moment it seemed
   As if I couldn't die.

AI IS NOT MY PASSION

I was invited to speak to a biology class at Nanjing University and wrote this song for the occasion

AI in is not my passion
Intelligent machines are hot
But not my fashion
I like genes and little white mice
Things that breathe, have feelings,
That's nice
It entices me.

AI is not the answer
Although it's true it may come through
And help us find a cure for cancer
It's really such a dangerous tool
And one that can cause so much strife
We're better off to put our emphasis on life
On life

AI or messy DNA
Diversity is more than okay
Life may seem in disarray
But babies beat out robots any day.

History, you're asking me,
I say it matters
Forget the past you'll find out fast
It's all collapsed
The future's left in tatters,
In tatters,
Inheritance, genetic code,
The color of your eyes
Is really history foretold,
Go forth and fertilize
Fertilize.

AI or messy DNA
Diversity is more than okay
Life may seem in disarray
But babies beat out robots any day.

The world is changing
Changing so fast
The status quo
It will not last
Here in the palm of your hand
The fate of humankind
The good news as I understand it
Is that fate is still undefined.

AI is not my passion

ALL I CAN THINK OF IS YOU

I'm in a taxi
Or I'm lying in bed
I'm on the telephone
Or eating toasted bread
I'm in a tie shop,
Shall I choose the blue or red?
All I can think of is you.

I must remember to watch
My favorite TV show
I should ring my mother
Just to say hello
I have to go to work
And sit there even though
All I can think of is you.

You're a ghost
That haunts me night and day
You're still with me
When the rest have gone away
I talk to you
As if you're here with me
If you do that too,
Must be telepathy.

I take an evening walk
Around the neighbourhood
I write out my To Do list
Like I know I should
But nothing I can do
Can do me any good
Cos all I can think of is you.

You're a ghost,
That haunts me night and day
You're still with me
When the rest have gone away
I talk to you
As if you're here with me
If you do that too,
Must be telepathy.

I've got to do the washing,
Go and pay some bills
Go to the store
To buy vitamin pills
But I won't go out
Looking for cheap thrills
Cos all I can think of is you, yeah
All I can think of is you
(no room for nothing else)
All I can think of is you
(that's all).

ALWAYS A WAY

They pushed you out,
I knew that they would
Never really a doubt,
Ah but it's all for the good.
You get so far,
Then you hit a brick wall
Listen you're a star,
It doesn't matter at all.

Thinking it through,
The joke's on them
You did good,
Without you mayhem.
You can't stop a fool,
From screwing it up
Don't lose your cool,
Just focus on the follow up

   There's always a way
   It'll all be okay
   There's always a way

Second acts,
They're part of life
Rewrite those contracts,
Create an afterlife
Persistence,
Now that's the key
Go the distance,
See what you will see.
Become what you will be

Do what I say, not what I do
I'm hoping my advice
Will help you not hurt you
Listen up, I don't want to
Lead you astray
Generally unless there isn't,
There's always a way

   There's always a way
   It'll all be okay
   There's always a way

ANOTHER LITTLE DRINK

I was looking for a party
Last Saturday night
I was looking my best
And I was feeling all right
Took a walk in the neighbourhood
Kept my ears peeled
For something sounding good
Well what do you think I found,
With my nose to the ground
It was a party.

Walked right in like
I knew the whole crowd
They were laughing and drinking
With the music real loud

Things looked good,
If you know what I mean
Kept my profile low,
I was checking out the scene.
I had a drink or four,
Or maybe several more
It was a party.

Another little drink
Before I throw up on the floor
Another little drink
Before they throw me out the door.

I smoothed right on
And headed straight for the bar
Dropped a hint that I was an
Incognito star
Said hello to a lady named Tess
Slipped and tripped
And split my drink all down her dress
She screamed and slapped my arms,
As I grabbed for her charms
Oh what a party.

Had a dance with two ladies in white
I said you're both beautiful
Won't you Come home for the night
The two ladies quickly merged into one
When a large man loomed,
Grabbed my neck and thereupon
Said who the hell are you,
I said Prince Andrew, how d'you do
Oh what a party.

Another little drink
Before I throw up on the floor
Another little drink
Before they throw me out the door.

ARMAGEDDON

The market's up
The market's down
Just wait a while
It goes round and round

I'm watching Bloomberg
And Reuters too
It's stock market carnage,
What am I going to do

My money's in the market
It's shrinking awful fast
I should have sold out last week
The good times couldn't last

My heart is beating faster
The end is getting near
Forget the fundamentals
All I feel is fear.

Perspective is the only
Benefit of age
I've seen it before
I'm sanguine if not sage
The market's up
The market's down
Just wait a while
It goes round and round

AS OLD AS YOU FEEL

Some days the sun is up there
Some days it goes who's knows where
But I'm always sunny
I guess it's kind of funny,
I always feel like a millionaire.

Mark Twain, now he was quite bright
He knew it wasn't simply black and white
He said, age is a matter
Of mind over matter
If you don't mind it don't matter.
He was right.

   We've all got our troubles
   In singles or in doubles
   Nobody is living the ideal
   But there'll always be an answer
   Barring hit-and-runs and cancer
   You're only as old as you feel.

You may say there's no way
To dodge the wheel of fate
Everything is strictly chronological
But relativity?
Well that makes good sense to me
I think I'd rather go with biological

Being young and healthy
And just a little wealthy
Ah now that would always be
The better deal
But there are so many reasons
To celebrate more seasons
You're only as old as you feel

It used to be if you were sixty-four
You couldn't count on very many more
But medical advances
Are widening our chances
I can live with that, oh that's for sure.

Anyway, I'm feeling kinda young
I feel like spring
Has only just this minute sprung
My knees may disagree
But that doesn't bother me
Complaints from body parts
Are left unsung.

   We've all got our troubles
   In singles or in doubles
   Nobody is living the ideal
   But there'll always be an answer
   Barring hit-and-runs and cancer
   You're only as old as you feel.

Can they stop the clock?
Ah now that would be a shock
That would change the world
For all who cared
Also, those who feel more old
End up dying first I'm told
So it's better to be mentally prepared.

   We've all got our troubles
   In singles or in doubles
   No one is living the ideal
   But there are many reasons
   To celebrate more seasons
   You're only as old as you feel.

BANG BANG BANG

I am an optimist. This is my optimist's anthem

There are days like this
When I just can't miss
When the world is on my side
It's the way to be
Infallibility
Now I can take that in my stride
On anything I've tried
On a day that simply glows
It's verified that
Everything just goes
Bang bang bang

It's not every day
That I feel this way
One in ten's not so bad, for sure
But I do persist
Cos I'm an optimist
I know there'll always be a cure
You can't call me insecure

I always do suppose
Tomorrow's another day when
Every last thing goes
Bang bang bang

I'm not a fool
I know exactly how things hang
It's not as if the world
Could hear that song I sang
Feeling this good
Could come back to hit me
Like a boomarang
But what the hell I'm feeling just like
Bang bang bang

I watch the stars
Beyond the bars
The door slams with a clang
My cell is cold
I won't be paroled
Forever on this chain-gang.
But wait! I spoke too soon!
I will be released at noon!
Bang bang bang!

I'm a lucky guy
I couldn't tell you why
But it's always been that way
May it long be so
But will it? I don't know
Tomorrow who can really say
My karma's good but hey
Gotta stay right on my toes
And catch that day
When everything still goes…
Bang bang bang

BETTER THAN

I took part in a six-week online writing course and wrote a song for each week. This was week six.

I don't write songs for a living
They're for giving, free to share.
I'm not after fame and fortune
One more tune or less
Is neither here nor there.

Anyway, words are overrated
Getting dated, body language says more
So why not go, wholly video
Make the best damn songs you never saw.

   Is it for attention (no)
   Or communication (no)
   A stab at immortality?
   Exercise the fingers?
   Training for the brain
   No, writing songs is simply better
   than watching TV.

Market demand is hardly buoyant
I'm not clairvoyant if I say it'll thrive
Tunes are not worth a dime a dozen
And hits are priced at less than a dollar 35.

But I still aim for prosody
Rhyme with ferocity,
Trying to make each phrase work
Writing songs, what a strange pursuit
But there's no substitute
If you have,
If you have the quirk.

Is it for attention (no)
Or communication (no)
A stab at immortality?
Exercise the fingers?
Training for the brain?
No, writing songs is simply better
Than watching TV

I told a lie
I really should clarify
Fame and fortune would be fine by me
If I qualify.

BIRD IN A CAGE

This is a true story. I met this old man dressed in ragged peasant clothes in front of a temple in the town of Tai'an at the base of Taishan mountain on a misty winter's day. He really did say "good afternoon" in English. And then he told me his story. I asked him how he felt and and he offered his assessment, which is the song name.

Swirls of mist hugged the mountainside
In a forest of stone
Round about, a dozen dragons hide
Cold to the bone
At the centre of creation
On the mountain of the gods
Temple eaves swooped down low and wide
I was almost alone, almost alone.

There he was, from another world,
An old peasant man
He was dressed, in ragged padded clothes
A deep, weathered tan
He smiled and in an Oxford accent
He said to me "good afternoon",
Across the gulf I asked him who he was
And he slowly began, slowly began.

When the world and I were younger,
I bid my home goodbye
Left the heartland of Confucius,
For the seaport of Shanghai.
But that didn't ease the hunger,
So I sailed the sea in ships
Felt the sun upon my shoulder,
Tasted salt upon my lips.

Oh, the places that I went to,
Oh, the sights, the things I did
Wonders that if I had stayed here,
Would have stayed forever hid.
I learned that life is full of sadness,
I learned that life is but a game
I learned that everyone is different,
I learned that we are all the same.

    We're birds in a cage.

Then the tides of history shifted,
Left me washed up on the shore
And the commissars they told me,
I could go to sea no more.
So I came back to this village,
Still I wasn't left alone
I was persecuted, beaten,
For the foreign things that I had known.

So the tide of red rolled onwards,
In its wake a million drowned
While the children of the Helmsman,
Rode the crest up to the mound.
Yes, they tried their best to cow me,
Those petty emperors of shame
On the outside they could chain me,
But inside I stayed the same.

    A bird in a cage.

For thirty years they kept me waiting,
And now my life is almost gone
And while I stayed here in this village,
The world outside was moving on.
No, I wouldn't say I'm bitter,
No, I'm not consumed by rage
I just envy those who stayed here,
They do not know we're in a cage

    That we're birds in a cage

CHOCOLATE FIX

I feel a choc-attack,
Sneaking up on me
That piece of chocolate cake
I was saving up for tea
Has got a come-hither look,
I just can't say no
It's brown, it's sweet, it's sticky,
Oh no, here I go.

   It's that time of the month,
   It's that time of the week
   It's that time of the day,
   When I have to say "Queek"
   I need a chocolate fix, yeah
   I need a chocolate fix, yeah
   I need a chocolate fix, yeah
   I need a fix or maybe five or six.

The time has come for me
To go and hit the bars
I'll have a Milky Way,
Or maybe a Mars
Neopolitan ice cream,
Is definitely fine

The vanilla and strawberry's for you,
The chocolate is all mine.

   I readily admit,
   That I love chocolate
   Oh yes I am obsessed,
   Cos chocolate's the best

   I need a chocolate fix, yeah ...
   I need a fix, that how I get my kicks.

   M & M's mean more to me than gems
   I want to be alone with a Toblerone

   I know it's crazy but,
   When I need chocolate
   I'd drive to anywhere,
   I just wouldn't care.

   I need a chocolate fix, yeah ...
   I need a fix or maybe five or six.

I've got a fatal fascination
For the sweeter things in life
You show me a piece of chocolate cake,
I'll show you a fork and knife
It's a serious addiction,
I no longer doubt it
I'm not chipping,
I'm fruit and nuts about it.

   It's that time of the month,
   It's that time of the week
   It's that time of the day,
   When I have to say "Queek"
   I need a chocolate fix, yeah ...
   I need a fix, I need a fix I need a fix
   I need a chocolate fix, yeah ...
   I need a fix, that's how I get my
   Chocolate kicks, yeah yeah.

You know where you are,
With a Hershey bar
Please oh please,
I want some multi-coloured Smarties ...

COME SEPTEMBER

This song was written to commemorate the coming birth of my daughter Jennifer in 1980

There are flowers in the air
There are flowers in your hair
There's a gentle swell,
And I know quite well
It means there's someone flowering there.

Be it boy or be it girl,
The child's as precious as a pearl
What will be its name,
Will things still be the same
It's sent my life into a whirl.

Come September I will have a protege
That twinkle in my eye
Last December had its way
Come September,
There'll be three of us to feed
Me and you, the baby too,
I'm certain we can make it through
One thing that I know is true
It's very well pedigreed.

Summer autumn, winter spring
The seasons turn the years take wing
People live and die
The generations fly
The chain's continued in Peking

A mesh of genes so broad and vast
Leads to the future from the past
The essence of our soul
Is in the child made whole
To represent us to the last.

    Come September I will have a protege
    That twinkle in my eye
    Last December had its way
    Come September,
    There'll be three of us to feed
    Me and you, the baby too,
    I'm certain we can make it through
    One thing that I know is true
    It's very well pedigreed.

Will it look like you or me
Will it grow up happily
All I'm certain of, I'll give it all my love
And a guitar when it is three.
I've been a son before it's true
But can I be a father too
Only time will tell, if I can do it well
The child will start the chain anew.

Chorus

CONCRETE BEAMS

A cloudless sky,
A steel-blue dome up above me
Just you and I,
I love you and you love me
The wind's a sigh,
On the lips of a new day
No need to try,
There are no words that I could say

   The mountainside
   Is shimmering with a thousand dreams
   While from above,
   The sun beats down,
   Just like concrete beams.

Would it be worth,
The scent the taste of your sweet kiss
If then the earth,
Could be knocked off its axis
I'd hold you tight,
I'd see what love that we could make
Except it might,
It may just unleash an earthquake.

Chorus

Nothing is quite as it seems
Just like Concrete beams
beat beat, beat the heat
Concrete beams
Corona corolla, definitely soilar
Concrete beams
Going to extremes....

COPYRIGHT
(IS FOR THE LIVING)

This is a tune from John Coltrane
Based on a 12-bar blues refrain
With a famous five-note phrase
Perfection comes in simple ways
And it always will remain
The genius of Coltrane.

I've added lyrics to his song
Plus a new beat, a little more strong
That doesn't mean I claim it as my own
The provenance is certainly well known
And it always will remain
The genius of Coltrane.

Do I have to ask to make this track?
Or throw it out if they don't get back?
What legal status should there be
In this digital century?
To sing this doesn't mean that I disdain
The rights of John Coltrane.

Copyright is for the living
Royalties are not for the dead.

Copyright was meant as encouragement
To give authors income supplement
Convince them to do another one
But that's not an option now for John
Coltrane would be forgiving
Cos copyright is for the living

Copyright is for the living
Royalties are not for the dead.

COCO LOCO

This was inspired by a beachside bar and restaurant on the island of Boracay

Far across the ocean
In a corner of the planet
There's a little island
Lying on a bed of granite
Things are pretty quiet there,
Business could be better
Altho the sand couldn't be more golden,
The water not much wetter

Hawkers armed with straw hats
Ply their trade out in the hot sun
Lurking round the corner
Is a guard armed with a shotgun
Troubled times in paradise,
The sun keeps right on shining
Not a cloud up in the sky,
They sure could use a silver lining

And as the evening sky glows
They sit among the shadows
And watch a B-grade movie
On the colour video
Outside a scene from van Gogh
It's Nature's own Tonight Show
Don't you know
There's only one place that you should
... Go

Coco Loco Coco, Coco Loco Coco
Coco Loco Coco, Coco Loco.

There's nothing like a light breeze
Under exploding palm trees
As you watch the ocean
Edging up the beach below
It's like a scene from van Gogh
It's Nature's own Tonight Show
Don't you know

There's only one place that you should
... Go

    Coco Loco Coco, Coco Loco Coco
    Coco Loco Coco, Coco Loco.

Living in a beach hut has its charms,
I wouldn't knock it
But paradise is nicer
When there's money in your pocket
Coups don't help to feed the kids,
Neither do volcanoes
You got no option but to go,
Whichever way the wind blows.

The tourists wander by
Soaking in those rays called solar
Coconuts up in the trees,
But the natives they drink cola
Everyday they thank the man,
Who thought up printed T-shirts
It's either that or they'd have to go,
And cater to the perverts.

Amid the fading deckchairs
Far from your darkest nightmares
Under the mounted horns,
Of a water buffalo
Not quite a scene from van Gogh
It's Nature's own Tonight Show
Don't you know
There's only one place that
You should go

    Coco Loco Coco, Coco Loco Coco
    Coco Loco Coco, Coco Loco.

CRICKET IN A BASKET

There's a cricket in a basket
He's unhappy, doesn't mask it
He'd rather be outside
Than be here with me
He's singing all alone
Though it's more the brittle moan
Of a long incarcerated detainee

No parole
In return for food and no strife
For the term of his natural life
He will be

In solitary confinement
With no hope of re-assignment
Back to his home in a tree.

So it goes, so it goes
So it goes for me

It could be that I'm reading
Too much into the sound of his pleading
But I think I know
Just what he's trying to say
I am certain he's aware
That he doesn't stand a prayer
As his quota of days slips away.

Oh I know
This basket maybe nice
But it's really a hell of a price
To pay

So I listen as he sings
With the friction of his wings
And wonder at the depths of his dismay

A chorus of crickets are singing in that tree
With a majesty that nothing can dethrone
But the cricket in the basket,
He yearns for harmony
He feels the same as me
That a solo has no value on its own

So it goes
So it goes
So it goes for me

CRITIQUE

I once took part in an online group to which people uploaded photographs and other creative products for comments and guidance by members. The operator of the group gave this song a B-minus score.

I poured my heart
Into the process of production
A storm of creative fire
Out came this song,
I wonder if It's done
Time to enquire.

It's a disposable and silly little number
A microscopic piece of art
So show me no mercy,
There's no controversy
Rip it right apart.

I'm feeling pretty damn copacetic
I like it but that's just me
I got the chords, lyrics, melody,
But what I lack is
Objectivity.

Don't hold back,
I want you to attack

Yes, give me all your
Comments and suggestions
On every single word and note
Reveal all the cracks,
Critique to the max
Go for the throat.

Chill, be still my beating ego
It's so nice to
Go through the wringer
As writer and singer
And get some advice.

I'm ready for a talk-to or a takedown
But no need to get too vexed
Constructive forever,
Destructive? Whatever
On to the next.

Oh no,
Here comes that feedback flood
Oh no,
Looks like it's judged a dud

It's possible it's not complete perfection
I concede that it might be flawed
I get it, indeed, there's really no need
To applaud.

Don't hold back,
I want you to attack

So thank you for the slings
And all the arrows
The candid barbs and the oblique
I dealt with the flak,
With no answering back
Critique

DIRTY OLD MAN

Written in the early 1980s. Probably unacceptable as a topic today.

I only bought her a chocolate malt
You can hardly say
That the rest was my fault
But they said was indecent assault
Where's the justice.

   You think it's easy
   Being a dirty old man
   Well you're wrong,
   Yeah you're wrong
   When the weather gets as cold as hell
   You can get icycles on
   Your ding-dong bell.

The Grinstead flasher is a friend of mine
We often go out walking
With a bottle of wine
The girls all squeal,
They must think we're divine
But then they run away.

   Chorus

Flashing's an art, it can give you a tan
Where few other professions can
But I don't like being called
A dirty old man
I'm not old.

   Chorus

ELEPHANTS

I have always liked doing kids' songs and this was an effort at it. The recorded version features a choir of around 20 kids. Written and recorded in the early 1990s.

Here come the elephants ...
Here come the elephants ...

Here come the elephants
Two by two
They've broken out
Of the local zoo
No one knows
What they're going to do
When the elephants go by
Two by two.

Here come the elephants four by four
They stamp down the avenue
Past our door
Where are they going,
We can't be sure
As the elephants go by four by four.

Here come the elephants
Six by six
They shake the shadows
And break the bricks
Trees are falling
Like pickup sticks
As the elephants go by
Six by six.

Here come the elephants
Eight by eight
Their trunks are trumpeting
Past the gate
You'll be squashed down flat
If you jump too late
When the elephants go by
Eight by eight.

French fries and bowties,
Elephants in the park
See-saws and bear paws,
Be home before it's dark
Campfires and vampires,
Elephants off to Rome
Blindman's buff they've had enough,
It's time to wander home.

There go the elephants
Ten by ten
They're going back
To the elephant's pen
They'll go to sleep
'til tomorrow then
They'll watch the people go
Ten by ten.

ELIZABETH

My daughter Jennifer had a doll with this name and she sang it. At about the age of 10

Elizabeth wants a doll
Her very own special doll
She wants it to cuddle,
She wants to brush its hair
She's got lots of clothes
That she wants it to wear
It's not me that wants it,
It's Elizabeth I swear
You know that you can trust me.

She wants pocket money like me
For when she goes out you see
She doesn't want much,
Just a little every day
Twenty-five dollars
Would be enough I'd say
Give it to me,
I'll put it safe away
You know tht you can trust me.

Elizabeth, Elizabeth
The doll with a mind of her own
Elizabeth, Elizabeth
What will she be like
When she's grown.

Elizabeth wants a pet
But she hasn't decided yet
Whether to choose
A puppy or a cat
She wants an animal
That she can stroke and pat
One thing I'm sure of,
She doesn't want a rat
And that's okay with me.

Chorus

Elizabeth is asleep (shhhhh!)
So be quiet, don't make a peep (shhhh!)
No, we shouldn't wake her,
Not yet anyway
She needs to take a nap
Cos she didn't yesterday

But when you've gone
She will wake up straight away
Cos it's time to play with me.

Chorus

EMPHASIS

This song was written for the online songwriting course.

If I get your drift,
A line is not defined
By the number of syllables
It contains
One or many,
The structure,
As i understand it,
Basically remains
The key to writing songs
Is pretty simple, More or less
Just work out the syllables,
That you have To stress

Primary stresses, secondary stresses
Do what you like but no stress excesses.

    Preserve the natural shape
    Of the language

If i understand you right,
Words are divided into four types,
There are the meaning words,
Like bagpipes and facewipes
And Jack Snipes,
And stars and stripes
These words should always be stressed,
To convey the meaning best
Don't let the grammaticals,
The pronouns, the prepositions,
Be anything but suppressed.

Primary stresses,
Secondary stresses
Do whatever you like
But do stress excesses

    Preserve the natural shape
    Of the language

The grammaticals in particular,
Are a base, like velvet so black
On which the flashing gems of our stories
Are laid out to shine back to back
Our job as songwriters,
If I might paraphrase
Is to organize the rhythms
Ready for the melody
And the actual phrase

    Preserve the natural shape
    Of the language

EVERYBODY HAS A PRICE

Everbody here has a price
Everybody wants an extra bowl of rice
Trying to make a million
By legal means of stealing.
Everybody here has a price.

It used to be that all the cops were bent
That's the way the Hong Kong story went
Raking in the money fast
They were sure their luck would luck
Counting on the cooperation of
    government.

Everybody here can be bought
I'm sure everyone has thought
If I was offered my weight in gold
Could I say no, could I be so bold
Everybody here can be bought.

See the girl in the black dress
What's her profession, let's see if you guess
She will make you feel alright
For a price she will stay all night
She's an actress.

Everybody here is bribable
I believe that everybody here is liable
To take a bribe if it's big enough
Damn morality and all that stuff
Everybody here is bribable.

But don't worry,
We're all the same
It's the cash that counts
Not from where it came
That's the Hong Kong philosophy
It works for you and it works for me
So don't worry,
We're all the same.

FAILURE

You know Van Gogh,
He only sold
One painting,
In his life, all told
But he wouldn't let it drop,
One ear or two, he wasn't gonna stop
Got to do another, he said,
It's the next one that'll pop.

    Woulda shoulda coulda,
    If only
    Woulda shoulda coulda,
    That's not for me

You see Mallory,
He tried his best
When he scaled that Himalayan peak,
Mount Everest.
As the ice flashed up towards him,
He thought, better not crash land
Next time, you know,
I think I'll grab that Yeti's hand.

    Woulda shoulda coulda,
    If only
    Woulda shoulda coulda
    That's not for me

Failure, yes failure, it'll nail ya
It'll pull you down, you run and it'll tail ya
But chase it, embrace the fact of failure
Take from each mistake, and it will never
    fail ya

    Woulda shoulda coulda,
    If only
    Woulda shoulda coulda,
    If only
    Woulda shoulda coulda,
    If only

I've tried success
I was learning less
You ask wise men
They'll say fail
And then fail
Again and again and again

Now it comes to,
Little me
The edge of success is
Familiar territory
I have learned
How to rhyme,
An achievement
Hardly rated as sublime
But with failure as my guide
There's still hope
And yes, there's still time.

Woulda shoulda coulda,
If only
Woulda shoulda coulda,
That's not for me
Woulda shoulda coulda,
If only
Woulda shoulda coulda,
That's not for me

FINISH THE RICE

I can see where is going
The prospect isn't pretty
The situation's out of hand
It's really such a pity
Why won't she just obey

The mother's getting mad
The dad is close to shouting
The kid simply sitting there
Fiddling and pouting
A war of wills
There's no middle way.

How to
Make you
Do exactly what I want you to do
Without appealing to those drivers
Fear and greed?
Success?
I guess
Is to get you from no to you
May as well just take the fifth and plead:

Finish the rice
And you can do anything
You can do anything
At all.

There are songs I have to write
Articles to edit
A book I have to read
So I can say that I have read it
So much is in the queue.
I collect all of the pieces
The basic information
Finishing is where I fail
It's pure procrastination
There's always
Something else to do.

To get me
To be
Exactly what I want me to be
I got to press that button
That's marked "dire need"
I know
It's slow

To get me to go to yes from no
I may as well just give it up and plead:

   Finish the rice
   And you can do anything
   You can do anything
   At all.
   Yeah finish the rice
   And you can do anything
   You can do anything
   At all.

You've got to think it through
Have to be inventive
Look at all the options
And find the right incentive
There are those who say
Pleading is not okay
But if there's no other way
Then I say, hey,
Okay…

Finish the rice
And you can do anything
You can do anything
At all.
Yeah finish the rice
And you can do anything
You can do anything
At all.
Yes, at all.

FLYING

You're looking really good
In that new green dress
It gets my blood a-racing,
It really does impress
My mind is moving over
The bumps and all the curves
Sure to grab attention,
Just as it deserves.

Now maybe I should buy
A new suit and tie
Something right
For a night out on the sly
But then again
It isn't a clothing competition
I am not a mannikin,
I don't qualify for that position

    Flying, up into the sky
    I'm flying too
    Sometimes low and sometimes high
    Flying, past the speed of sound
    Oh but then we met again,
    Back down on the ground.

I really like the way
You're moving when you walk
If beauty is a package deal,
You walk the walk and talk the talk
Your lovely eyes, your thighs,
The list goes on and on
I am appreciative,
I must confess my self-control is gone.

The years go by,
They only make you better
The word entrancing,
Now that suits you to the letter
I hope you will forgive me,
I'm laying it all out
The planets all align,
There isn't any doubt.

    Flying, up into the sky
    I'm flying too, sometime low and
    Sometimes high
    Flying, past the speed of sound
    On but then we met again,
    Back down on the ground.

FOOL I WAS

Relax, he said to me
This can't go wrong
They signed a guarantee
Everything's okay
Just wire the cash
By close of biz today.

It's really in the bag
I simply cannot spot
A single snag
Once the money's there
Before you know it
you're a millionaire

    Fool I was ...

He slapped me on the back
He said with me
You're on the inside track
I've got the deal in hand
Although it may be hard
To understand

What was I to say
A meal I was before
This bird of prey
I signed the dotted line
And gave away
The bulk of what was mine.

The fool thinks he is wise
The wise man knows himself
To be a fool
I'd like to think I'm wise
But then I've always thought
I'm kind of cool.

FRONT PAGE LEAD

I wrote this song in honour of the news editor of the South China Morning Post in the early 1970s, Kevin Sinclair. A New Zealander. What a character!

It's a scoop, it's a story,
It's got drive, it's got speed
It's a shock horror drama,
That'll make your poor heart bleed
It's a must, stop the presses,
Oh, now this you've got to read
It's a ball-tearing monster,
It's a front page lead.

You've got to get the facts right
And you've got to write it quick
Just add a few fast cliches
And it's bound to read real slick
You may wonder how one judges
If a story's really hot
Does it grab you by the short and hairies?
Write it on the spot.

It's said the subs are there
To stop the errors creeping in
It seems to me they're there
To help the dreaded gremlin
The way they spike and mutilate
My stories shows they're fiends
Sub stands not for sub-editor,
Sub-human's what it means.

Chorus

Before you all decide
You want to be a journalist
You've got to learn to drink your fill
And more and not get pissed
The job consumes your interest,
Can consume your life as well
The burnt-out journalist
Lives in a special kind of hell.

But the dinky-di reporter
Chases stories till he drops
While there's news left to be written,
You can bet he never stops
Even when the paper's put to bed
And the presses spring to life
You'll find the true-blue journalist
Still screaming to his wife:

    It's a scoop, it's a story,
    It's got drive, it's got speed
    It's a shock horror drama,
    That'll make your poor heart bleed
    It's a must, stop the presses,
    Oh, now this you've got to read
    It's a ball-tearing monster,
    It's a front page lead.

GETAWAYS

A steamy day in the city
Traffic's manic, it's not at all pretty
Tempers rising up to meet the heat
The cars just sit there, going nowhere
Drivers sweating,
They want to get somewhere
Anywhere but trapped here on this street.

    In a dust and fume filled haze
    We watch the sun go down
    We dream of getaways
    (I wanna get away)
    Oh we wonder why we stay
    To see the world run down
    Then shrug and sigh and say,
    There's no escaping anyway.

The traffic moves, inching slowly
Engines gunning, a chorus unholy
Air-conned capsules looking for a break
(out, breakout)
A siren wails, the kids are crying
In the background, the radio's lying
Saying something about the love we make.

There's an eagle, he's gliding overhead
He's gazing at the traffic from on high
There's a driver, in the traffic,
He's looking up
He wishes he could fly,
Like the eagle to the sky

In a dust and fume-filled haze
We watch the sun go down
We dream of getaways
(I wanna get away)
Oh we wonder why we stay
To see the world run down
Then shrug and sigh and say
There's no escaping anyway.

GO NOW

You love him you suppose
The problems aren't all of his making
He's the one you chose
Am I the only one that sees you're faking.

The silence full of words
You prefer to leave unspoken
No promises were made or heard
Your heart's the only thing
That's been broken.

   You can say that
   It's none of my business
   You'll live your life
   The way you know how
   The decision is yours,
   Just as it's his
   But I would suggest you
   Go now.

He works nights and you work days
In between you sometimes see him
The future's past, the present's haze
The dreams you had,
Have grown dim, grown dim.

The laughter that has died
The children that he doesn't want born
The tears you haven't cried
Meanwhile time is
Moving on, moving on.

   Chorus

GOOD BETTER BEST

This song is about the dilemma of parenthood. Kids are the best and the worst at the same time.

Unbelievably good,
Always does what she should
She's just great, no debate
Except when she isn't.

Indisputably nice
She's a steal at any price
What a star, she'll go far
Unless she doesn't.

Success is not a cert for anyone
That silver spoon
Can fall out of your mouth
But if you try your best
To be better than the rest
Then you can make it anywhere
East or west, north or south.

Unbelievably good,
Always does what she should
She's just great, no debate
Except when she isn't.

Good is not good enough
But it's a start
When the going's getting rough
You gotta take heart
Don't shy away from any test
Listen to me and pay attention
That helps memory retention
Then you just do what I suggest
Power through
Good and better to best.

Categorically smart
On the ball right from the start
She's as quick as a slick
Except when she isn't.

GOOD NIGHT

A lullaby

Good night, sleep tight
It's the end of another day
Don't let the bedbugs bite
Tell them all, to go away.

Good night, everything's all right
I'll see you in the morning
Just after the sky turns bright
And a new day is dawning.

   Picture a willow, a beautiful tree
   Down by a chattering stream
   Lie on your pillow
   And then count to three
   Off you head into a dream

Good night, there's no reason to fight it
Close your eyes, and let go
Feeling light, like a kite
Under the moon's silver glow

Lie in the sweet arms of slumber
And try to count all of the sheep
Before you can reach a high number
Off you will go into sleep.

Good night, sleep tight
It's the end of the day
Don't let the bedbugs bite
Tell them all to go away
Tell them all to go away
Tell them all to go away.

GORBY IS A CIA SPY

Written in 1990

Communism is on the run,
Pushed aside by everyone
Poland, Hungary and Rumania,
Czechoslovakia and Germania
I've got some information,
Provides an explanation
For this extraordinary
Epoch-making situation
My information comes from
Sources close to Red Square
So keep it close don't blab it anywhere.

    Gorby is a CIA spy, no lie
    That's why communism's gonna die
    Gorby's on our side, I can confide
    That's why democracy's
    Had such an easy ride.

He was planted there by Washington
After World War Two was won
Left to burrow underneath the Soviet State
Around the world he tops the polls
He's also best of Langley's moles
The White House is ecstatic,
It sure was worth the wait, cos

    Chorus

The Eastern European states
Economies in dire straits
Were ready for an end
To Marx and Lenin for sure
But these were minor factors
We should not let them distract us
The reason why the communists
gave in without a war, is that

    Chorus

This may sound like a strange theory
But I pray you please to hear me
The evidence I have
Comes from a source of high rank
Every month the U.S. pays
A cash amount that would amaze
Into his account at the HongKong Bank.

   Chorus

But there's a twist I must relate
Gorbachev he couldn't wait
He became a double agent
Right from the start
He recruited then a lady spy
In Washington she now rides high
She keeps a candle burning for him
Deep in her heart.

Yeah Barbara Bush is a Soviet spy, no lie
That's why Gorbachev
Is such a happy guy
Barbara has a heart of red,
That's what I said
So George don't have to
Look for Commies
Underneath the bed.

GOVERNOR'S BLUES

In 1977, Hong Kong's anti-corruption organization the ICAC started going after all the police, and the police threatened to mutiny. The PLA were on the border ready to come over, a fact not reported at the time. The British did a deal. This song was mildly controversial at the time and elicited a big reaction from the crowd at the Old China Hand on Lockhart Road, many of whom were expat police inspectors. One night, the phone rang at just the right moment.

We let them all off,
It just had to be
We were faced with
A full blown police mutiny
I put all my faith
In the ICAC
But we still had to give them
Their damned amnesty.

    I've got the Governor's blues
    I'm sick of the whole bloody thing
    Ordered around
    By a bunch of young cops
    I'm just waiting for Peking to ring

We threatened the bribery
On which crime depends
They thought that we'd cut off
The stream of tens
That flows from the brothels
And opium dens
Oh I wish I was back in
Those old Scottish glens.

I've got the Governor's blues
I'm sick of the whole bloody thing
Ordered around
By a bunch of young cops
I'm just waiting for Peking to ring

It was once one November,
The day I remember
They held me to ransome that day.
They said we have the guns
And the police stations
And it's us or hello PLA.

In government house
As I called for the waiter
I turned to my old trusted colleague
Jack Cater
I asked him if this mess
Could ever be greater
He said, "Well Sir Murray,
Just wait until later."

I've got the Governor's blues
I'm sick of the whole bloody thing
Ordered around
By a bunch of young cops
I'm just waiting for Peking to ring

GREEN SO GREEN

A reaction to all the rice fields I saw in the summer of 2006 in Jiangsu and Anhui on my walk across China.

There's a green, a green
A green so green
It's the greenest green
I've ever seen
The paddy fields
The paddy fields.

It's a green, a green
It's a green so green
It's the greenest green
I've ever seen
It's in the paddy fields

It moves, it grooves
Excites, delights
It's life, a knife
So green it bites
The paddy fields

There's a sun, the sun
It's the sun, our sun
It's beaming down on everyone
And the paddy fields
The paddy fields.

It's a green, a green
It's a scene so green
Cos the sun beats down
Makes the green so green
In the paddy fields.

HE WHO DIES WITH MOST TOYS WINS

I often wondered
About the meaning of life
Why we put up
With all this trouble and strife.

I looked at Buddha
And Christianity
But something there told me beware
This is not the one for me.

Then I found it
By the glow of a green LCD
Yes, finally, it came to me
The true philosophy.

He who dies with most toys wins
Spend some money, your life begins
No one's counting
Good deeds bad sins
Counting possessions,
The rich man grins
Cos he who dies with most toys wins.

Gimme gadgets
With flashing coloured lights
Hifi gear stacked up to here's
One of the world's most moving sights.

The perfect plaything
Isn't cuddly, curvaceous or round
It's digitised, it's computerised
It's got stereo sound surround.

So choose your toys, boys
They can bring enlightenment
My car CD, believe you me
Was surely heaven sent.

It's leap of faith time
But don't forget the remote
Believe like me in electricity
Immortality doesn't come for free.

   He who dies with most toys wins
   Spend some money, your life begins
   No one's counting
   Good deeds bad sins
   Counting possessions,
   The rich man grins
   Cos he who dies with most toys wins.

HIGHWAY 318
(TO THE TUNE OF ROUTE 66)

Another song related to my walk across China, which started in 2004. Much to it was along Highway 318, which stretches west from Shanghai all the way through Chengdu to Lhasa.

If you ever plan
To travel west
Take my road,
The highway that's the best
Cast your fate on Highway 318.

It winds from Shanghai
To Chengdu
There's a lot of crazy places
To pass through
Cast your fate on Highway 318.

Now go go through Suzhou
On through Changzhou
Yichang city looks less than pretty
Oh see the Three Gorges
Dabieshan and Huzhou
Nanchong and Yuexi

Don't forget Huangpi
Tongling Nanling
Chongqing and Wanzhou

Won't you get hip to this timely tip
When you make that cross China trip
Cast your fate on Highway 318

Won't you get hip to this timely tip
When you make that cross China trip
Lose some weight out on Highway 318
Procreate out on Highway 318
But cast your fate on Highway 318.

HONGKONG BLUES
(100,000 CON MEN)

This song, about the near-mutiny of the Hong Kong police force in 1977, was a favorite of the Old China Hand crowd in the late 1970s, many of them expat policeman

There's a lease on the colony
It runs out pretty soon
In 1997, in July, or is it June
It doesn't really matter
They'll take it anyway
They could leave us til next century
Or walk right in today.

    Hongkong keeps on rolling
    Money oils the wheels
    There's a 100,000 con-men here
    A 100,000 deals.

We're the biggest orange eaters
We drink more brandy too
We got over-crowding
But you ought to see the view.
There's hot nights, and gang fights
And San Miguel beers
We got silver cloud Rolls Royce's
Coming out of our ears.

There's nothing in the future
There's nothing in the past
The disposable city
Nothing's built to last
It's hazy, it's crazy
Everyone's mad
But taking off from Kai Tak
Always makes me sad.

    Hongkong keeps on rolling
    Money oils the wheels
    There's a 100,000 con-men here
    A 100,000 deals.

HOUSEHOLD WARES

> A true story. I met this guy in a little nothing mountain village in southern Anhui on my walk across China. Surnamed Jiang, he was running a small shop. I made up the bit about him saying he couldn't get married.

I sell soft drinks, apples and pears
Alcohol and cigarettes, and other
Household wares
I've sat behind this counter since i was six
I don't get far beyond this stool,
Without my walking sticks
Without my walking sticks.

You offer to buy a pear from me,
I'll give it to you
You say that you don't want it,
Unless you pay me too.
My reply is if you pay, the pear
I will not give
My courtesy trumps your pity,
That's the way I live.
Yes, that's the way I live.

The sun shines on us all,
It will always be
The stars are no brighter,
For you than for me
I have no envy,
You've got problems too
At least I don't have to pretend
To be perfect
Perhaps you do.

    I can fly, to the edge of imagination
    I can fly, wherever my inner eye can see
    I can fly, it's a validation
    Of what's beyond what you behold
    Let's call it, the real me.

I remember when I was 10,
My mother taught me to smoke
She hoped it would ease the pain,
It made me cough and croak
Now here I am, I'm 28,
And a husband I'll never be
But when it comes to cigarettes,
My best customer is me
My best customer is me

The sun shines on us all,
It will always be
The stars are no brighter, for you …

I can fly, to the edge of imagination
I can fly, wherever my inner eye can see
I can fly, it's a validation
Of what's beyond what you behold
Let's call it, the real me.

A few years later, he called me, and I told him I'd written a song about him.
"Just to be sure," I said, "did you ever get married?"
"Oh yes," he replied. "My brother died, so I married his widow to make sure his daughter had a father."
A human being on a different level.

HOW SHOULD I SAY IT

The sun was shining like a light
A picture postcard view in sight
The wind felt like an electric fan
The earth was the colour of a good deep tan.

    How should I say it
    I can't find the words
    Or the right turn of phrase
    How should I say it
    I want to express myself
    In a thousand different ways
    In poems and plays
    In books that amaze
    In conversational blues greens reds whites blacks and greys.

The grass was green as lime ice cream
The girl by my side was like a dream
She had all of a doll's sweet charms
Skin as smooth as Barbie's arms.

How should I say it
My tongue is twisted
And my lips are tied
How should I say it
If I could think of a witty remark
I'd be home and dried
On the right side
With no need to hide
The fact is that all my brain cells
Have been fried.

I CARE

In 1994, I released a CD of some of my songs for sale through the Body Shop in Hong Kong. It was called I Care and was dedicated to environmental issues and saving tigers

Wake up, and smell the air we're breathing
See the blanket smothering us all
A line of grime from here to the horizon
Could our own successes bring our fall.

   Do we have to kill, all of mankind
   To save the world, leave it all behind?
   Oh no, it can't be too late,
   It cannot be our fate
   To suffocate our Mother Earth,
   Through childish oversight,
   Now wait, we still have time to spare
   No reason to despair, just say I care.

Look down, deep into the waters
The scum of Humankind is rising high
See what we bequeath our sons and daughters
A world in which the seas are left to die

   Do we have to kill, all of mankind
   To save the world, leave it all behind

Beaches dying, cities choke,
Forests bleed
Rivers poisoned, mountains stripped,
All indeed
In the name of plain simple greed.

Now wait, we still have time to spare,
No reason to despair, just say I care.
It can't be too late, it cannot be our fate,
To suffocate our Mother Earth,
Through childish oversight,
Now wait, we still have time to spare
No reason to despair, just say
I care.

I LIKE THE RAIN

A jazz lyric

There's something very special
About the patter
Of rain on a window pane
Each drop makes a tentative plop
And erases the strain from my brain.

There are those who I believe
Would beg to differ
Who see rain as a curtain of tears
I say though the day may be gray
The wetness is fine 'til it clears.

It falls in squalls from thunderclouds
That entertain
Or dribbles down in showers
That tranquilize
In Spain the rain may mainly fall
In plain disdain
In here, it's just a sight for sore eyes.

So it may disrupt the flights
And downtown traffic
But you won't hear me complain
I'm dry and that's probably why
I like the rain.

I'M ME

I stole the Sting line from an Australian poet. I wrote to him and apologized, sent him the song. He ignored me, but also didn't sue

It's true that I am not James Brown
But I don't let it bring me down
No offense, but screw James Brown
I'm me I'm me I'm me

Clearly I am not Brad Pitt
I don't care even a little bit
Who needs all of that media shit
Not me not me not me

I don't deny I'm not Jay-Z
I wouldn't ever want to be
There's no need to pity me
I'm me I'm me just me

I'm happy being who I am
There's not much choice, it's true
For you the deal is just the same
You're you you're you you're you

I guess I never can be Sting
He's taken every breath
I'm not jealous, I can sing
Oh Sting, where is thy death?

I'M JUST SAYING

An anthem for China watchers

Is this place stable or unstable
I analyse it just as much as I am able
I'm trying to get a sense
Of what is going on
You can say it's stable
Cos congress come and congress gone.

    I'm not saying this place is tough
    Not saying it's obscure
    I'm just saying …

I see the depth, the scope of it all
My head, it's in a spin
I like the drama the potential's not small
I'm in …

I'm not saying this place is tough
Not saying it's obscure
Not saying I've had enough
Not saying that for sure.
I'm just saying …

Transparency, is good to see
My eyes are peeled for stable meritocracy
But I've decided I won't let it bother me
Where would I be without inscrutability.

Just one voice, therefore unstable …
But the GDP just grows
And grows
And grows
And grows,
It must be stable.

    I'm not saying this place is tough
    Not saying it's obscure
    Not saying I've had enough
    Not saying that for sure
    I'm just saying …

IT DOESN'T GET BETTER

Don't play it too safe in life....

I've spent all my life building castles
Cathedrals of clouds in the air
I tell myself that it doesn't matter
They seem so real when they're there

I don't worry about failure
Cos I don't try to succeed
I tell myself things are fine as they are
I have all that I need.

   It doesn't get better than this
   It doesn't get better,
   This side of a kiss
   But kissing is dangerous,
   Best to resist
   It doesn't get better than this.

I'm waiting for nothing and no one
I've had what I need all along
The beauty of anticipation
Is never to prove yourself wrong

I don't believe what's in the papers
I ignore what I see on the screen
This is the best that it ever could be
The best that it has ever been.

   Chorus

   The best of all possible worlds…

   Chorus

IT'S FAKE

There's a context to this song which for various reasons I am not at liberty to explain for a couple more years

I buy a glass of milk
It tastes so sweet, as smooth as silk
(It's fake)
See those cuddly toys,
For all the girls and boys
(They're fake)

Auto parts and cheese
Gurus and listed companies
(They're fake)
Works of art and jade
Handbags, watches, all custom-made.
(They're fake)

I'm in favor of nuance
And make-believe
Embellishments, refinements
And dreams
But it would be nice, at least with milk
If everything was just as it seems.

I choose a famous wine
The after-taste is less than divine
(It's fake)
This porcelain's exquisite
It sure looks real, but is it.
(It's fake)

Smart phones and cigarettes
Promises of fiscal rigor
(They're fake)
Details in CVs
Body parts with sass and vigor.
(They're fake)

   Chorus

Rice and chewing gum
Marmalade, Jamaican rum
(They're fake)
Banknotes and facial cream
Batteries, a truly benevolent
One-party regime.
(It's fake)

Bridges, trains and schools
Reliable Chinese statistics
(They're fake)
Pharmaceuticals and jewels
Assorted cancer-curing mystics.
(They're fake)

   I'm in favor of nuance
   And make-believe
   Embellishments, refinements
   And dreams
   But it would be nice, at least with milk
   If everything was just as it seems.

IT'S GOOD TO SEE YOU

A song I wrote to welcome people listening to me sing in a bookshop coffee bar on a Saturday afternoon…The melody to the song is the Family Mart convenience store jingle.

Hey it's good to see you,
I'm so glad you came
If that chair was empty,
Wouldn't be the same
As I walked on over,
I hoped that you'd be here
Great that you could make it,
Come to lend an ear
I got songs, yes quite a few
I'm delighted I can sing them for you
Hey it's good to see you,
I'm so glad you came

It's another Saturday
Nothing much else to do anyway
Hey it's good to see you,
I'm so glad you came
So glad ... So glad ...

Music live's fantastic
Utterly non-plastic
But need an audience there's no doubt
Thanks for coming out

Hey it's good to see you,
I'm so glad you came
If that chair was empty,
Wouldn't be the same
While I'm singing to you,
Just relax in your chair
You hear the call of nature,
Toilet's over there
I got songs, yes quite a few
I'm delighted I can sing them for you
Hey it's good to see you,
I'm so glad you came

KARMA

There are people out there
They really don't care
They steal and they lie
Then simply deny.

    There's not a religion
    To which I cleave
    But I choose to believe
    In karma.

Seen a lot of bad deals
Know just how it feels
Watched evil unfold
People bought and then sold.

    There's not a religion
    To which I cleave
    But I choose to believe
    In karma.

Revenge on delay
But it's coming your way
You won the first round
But watch the rebound.

    There's not a religion
    To which I cleave
    But I choose to believe
    In karma.

LADY ROAD

I'm tearing down your dotted line,
Loving your soft shoulders
There's no speed limit in this loading zone,
There's no lights to hold us.
It's a love affair so sweet and rare,
Blessed by the driving code
Your smooth grey skin did me in,
I'm in love
With Lady Road.

Your freeway spirit turns me on,
There's no waiting for an answer
Lying before me so slim and sleek,
Curved like a dancer
You've been used by many men before,
You're a tramp as it's been showed
But I've no right turn and no turn left,
I'm in love
With Lady Road.

    With Lady Road, Lady Road,
    Lady Road, Lady Road
    Lady Road, Lady Road, Lady Road,
    I said Lady Road.

I'm overtaking much too fast,
I see detours up ahead
I see you shake your head and smile,
As the traffic lights turn to red
I've gone too far to slow down now,
There's no way to ease this load
No parking or waiting or standing around,
I'm in love
With Lady Road.

LANTERNS

The inspiration for this lyric was a book by the great China writer Jonathan Spence called *Return to Dragon Mountain*. The year is 1644, the place is Shaoxing in eastern China, the dynasty is falling apart and the Manchus are about to invade. It took them a year to take over the whole country, but in the meantime, our narrator (Zhang Dai) wants to have another drink.

The possible end of an empire
Far away from here
The sun is descending, behind the hills
But the wine is still warm and clear.
Big pieces moving on the chessboard
May impact on me some day
For now It's all beyond me,
I'm heading out to dine and play.

The rustle of silk
As the girls make way
Semi-circled fans in their hands,
They sway
The lanterns light the way.

I'm off to consult with the Muses
An idle and arguable game
No matter the tricks revealed by the sticks
Things seem to work out much the same.
Floating in a sea of incense,
Espying the outlines of fate
If they're coming, why not come quickly,
The Muses say be patient and wait.

The rustle of silk
As the monks make way
Counting out the beads in their hands,
They sway
The lanterns light the way.

I've always worked hard
To avoid reality
I've succeeded for so long
But it's catching up with me.

We dine on an elegant houseboat
Moored just a skip from the shore
I remember the moment distinctly
Because I will see it no more.
The warmth of the evening entices,
I make my excuses and leave
The forecourt is covered with blossoms,
Fragile and fallen, they grieve.

The rustle of silk
As the girls make way
Semi-circled fans in their hands,
They sway
The lanterns light the way.

LEAVING HOME TODAY

We packed up all the knick-knacks,
And turned off the TV
We gave the cat away
We tied up all the loose ends,
The bank accounts, old friends
We're leaving home today.

We had a farewell party,
The family were all there
We got a silver tray
The kids are none to happy,
They don't understand why
We're leaving home today.

Tell us why
   We're doing it for you
Why we fly
   It'll all be okay
Home is here
   You know we adore you
Near is dear
   We're leaving today.

We loaded up the taxi
And flew to the airport
We're really on the way
The kids were in the back
With their pocket Nintendo
We're leaving home today.

The luggage isn't locked yet,
My god where's the tickets
I wonder should we stay
Yes I know I'm joking,
There's no turning back now,
We're leaving home today.

    Chorus

Oh we make ourselves strangers there
Searching for better days
For our children we hope and dare
We'll be better off there
Than anybody who stays.

So now we're in Toronto,
We live in the suburbs,
I guess we're doing okay
The young one's drinking milk,
Says he wants to turn snow white,
What else is there to say?

How are things at home,
Hope you're all keeping well now,
We'll visit you in May
The kids are none too happy,
They can't understand why,
We're going home some day.

    Chorus

LET'S SAMBA

Break out,
The coloured T-shirts
The bermuda shorts
And the floppy long skirts.
Look up,
A strange yellow thing
Has appeared in the sky
After so much grey rain.

    Let's samba, don't ask me how
    My feet want to dance
    And they want to start now
    Caramba, I suddenly find
    Brazilian rhythms
    Have captured my mind
    Let's samba, let's samba
    Yeah, let's samba.

Get down,
And shuffle your feet
There's places to go
And people to meet
Come on,
The smile on your face
Says you've decided you're part
Of the whole human race.

    Chorus

Look out,
My feet have gone wild
If I step on your toes
Please don't get riled
Good grief,
I'm losing control
The carnival spirit
Has stolen my soul.

    Chorus

LIFE AND DEATH

This question of life and death.
It hangs over us quietly
Gaining in contrast as the years go by
I decided long ago, to ignore it.

What would be the point
Of paying attention
Acknowledging its presence,
Allowing it to guide my actions?

Live life as if every day was your last
That makes sense
But it's not the same as saying
I'm afraid of dying.

But I do assume that life
Is better than the alternative
Though there's no way to prove it
One way or another.

The big questions
The Afterlife, Heaven, God
These are best left to philosophers.
There are no answers.

So back to life, back to life.

I see myself on a plateau
Walking on a plateau,
A wide and silent plateau
And I will stay on this path
For as long as i can.

No bell curve for me,
Thank you very much.
Aiming at 200, aiming at 200,
As a minimum, and why not?

I'm an optimist
And that in itself is a choice
I could choose to be a pessimist
But to what purpose?

I know deep down inside of me
That I'm really 28
Which is one year older
Than I was five years ago
So I cannot be accused
Of ignoring
The march of time.

To sum up,
I intend to live forever
Or die in the attempt.

MAN'S BEST FRIEND

A comment on the amount of dog shit I espied on the streets of French cities. Maybe it has changed since this 1980s, maybe not

My friends, I must mention,
A topic of dissension
I don't wish to anger or to nauseate
But lately I have found,
A rising tide of brown around
It is something I think we should regulate.

People of sophistication,
In every single nation
Let their avenues of style go to the dogs
To be entirely factual,
Their dogs do what is natural
And the rest of us
Must walk through doggy bogs

Yes if you miss then you're in it
You might as well bear and grin it
But don't get browned off
By those blues
Just tell yourself you've got
Two-tone shoes

And thank Man's Best Friend
(At the other end)
Man's Best Friend
(At the other end)
Man's Best Friend
(At the other end)
The north end of a south-bound dog
Is what offends.

To a dog there's nothing sweeter,
Than a whiff of some excreta
Each pile an aromatic calling card
With side-steps and jumps,
You negotiate the lumps
Don't be caught
Off your canine doodoo guard

I don't mean to be faecetious,
But this issue ought to teach us
Something of the owners
Whom these pets obey
For those with morals drooping,
Who won't stoop to pooper scooping
I suggest that we flush them all away.

    Chorus

MARY CORRIGAN

Mary was born in Ireland and was the mother of my father's second wife. She was, as the song suggests, angelic.

Mary Corrigan,
Go on take a bow
I know you're modest,
But you deserve it anyhow
I want to tell you,
This won't come as a surprise
In the game of life
You've been awarded first prize.

    Oh, everybody agrees
    You're the best, the bumble bee's knees
    Oh Mary Corrigan, it cannot be denied
    That the angels are on your side.

Mary Corrigan,
You're unselfishness made real
You beat saints Peter, Paul and Mary,
In the pursuit of the ideal
You always have a joke to tell,
Or a piece of good advice
I hate to use the word,
But you're just so damn nice.

Chorus

Mary Corrigan,
You've had your share of pain
But you've given out more love,
Than half a dozen lives contain
You raised a family,
The kids turned out okay
Their kids have got their own kids now,
Thanks to you they're on their way.

Chorus

    I hope you don't mind this song
    It'll be over, before too long
    I wouldn't want to embarrass you
    But you know that every word is true.

Mary Corrigan,
I know you're not averse
To a little glass of something,
To help to quench a little thirst
When you get to the gates
Where St Peter waits all day
I know he'll give you such a hug
And then he'll raise his glass and say:

Oh, everybody agrees
You're the best, the bumble bee's knees
Oh Mary Corrigan, it cannot be denied
That the angels are on your side.

The angels are on your side
The angels are on your side.... (fade)

ME AND THE MULTITUDES

Here am I
All in all I'm a pretty patient guy
Waiting calmly, yes waiting quietly
For the call.

I'm prepared
Through the years I have never once
despaired
Waiting calmly
For success, nothing less
The lavish praise, and bouquets
For

My desire
Is simply this, to amaze and to inspire
Then bathe my ego
In the rush, the paparazzi crush
Then sail along
A carpet that was laid for
Me, Just for me.

You may say, so will they
Chasing fame is such a cliche
That may be, I agree
But all or nothing, there's no half way

   Me and the multitude
   Just for me, the applause
   Me and my throngs of fans
   Every one of whom, adores

Me, and the multitude
Me and the applause
Me and my throngs of fans
Every one adores…

I'm still here
A simple guy I hope that that is clear
Waiting calmly,
Yes waiting quietly
For the call.

MID-LIFE CRISIS

Well here I am, I'm half way through
I'm on my own, left to my own devices
I've thought about it, I've decided
That I will not have a mid-life crisis.

    Everything is going fine,
    I'm in a good mood most the time
    I'm on top of everything,
    That's the reason I can sing
    All I've got to do is sing,
    There's nothing to fear
    Nothing to fear.

I've been around, I know the score
I'm old enough to know
Just what the price is
I've weighed the odds and worked it out
There is no reason for
A mid-life crisis.

The year's go by, it's no big deal,
I've no big problems to conceal
Nothing's really changed at all,
I see no writing on the wall
I'm certain I'm winning,
The future is clear
You see that I'm grinning,
There's nothing to fear
Nothing to fear.

I'm looking good and doing great
I've made a pact,
There'll be no compromises
No explosions, no disasters
All under control,
No mid-life crisis.

I've got a few grey hairs it's true,   I will not have a mid-life crisis,
But I feel like I used to do   ... will not have a mid-life crisis
Sometimes I'm gazing into space,   ... will not have a mid-life crisis
Just say it once more to my face   ... will not have a mid-life crisis

I'm certain I'm winning,
The future is clear
You see that I'm grinning,
There's nothing to fear
Nothing to fear.

MY OWN TWO FEET

A job does not define you
A title even less
Degrees and acronymed guarantees
Don't impress.

I once got a college tie
To bolster my career
Then I realized, privilege disguised
It was just a veneer.

   I stand on my own two feet
   Even if the balance is incomplete
   You'll get no argument from me
   This is how it was meant to be.
   Just my own two feet
   The ones I use out on the street
   What you see is what you get
   Not a silhouette ....

How to process wealth and fame
When you're just a kid
That's a challenge some folks have
But I never did

Here we are, islands in the stream
But not as separate as we seem
Underneath the water is more land
I've been criticized for many things
But this I do understand
Don't refuse a helping hand.

I stand on my own two feet
Even if the balance is incomplete
You'll get no argument from me
This is how it was meant to be.
Just my own two feet
The ones I use out on the street
What you see is what you get
Not a silhouette ....

Clouds have silver linings
Black can turn to white
Every problem can be solved
I know that's right
It must be right.

NEVER MORE THAN NOW

I remember, you fast asleep
When you were young
The sound of your breathing more magical
Than any song, that was ever sung

Then years later, on a mountain road
You and me, walking through the day
An aura of enchantment encompassed you
Blew them all away.

   More than the laughter
   More than the rush
   Of thrills that seemed so intense
   But really just made no sense
   Even at first blush
   More than excitement
   More than the wow
   I appreciate the little things
   The little joys that living brings
   Never more than now.

Another verse, another story
This one of giggling and three
That was your age
And that was the number
I was lucky that the three included me.

What is beauty, what endures
Is not the glow of youth
It's not a face, or even grace
I think that beauty's probably just truth.

   More than the laughter
   More than the rush
   Of thrills that seemed so intense
   But really just make no sense
   Even at first blush
   More than excitement
   More than the wow
   I appreciate the little things
   The little joys that living brings
   Never more than now.

Now is the time, to find a rhyme
Without admitting high crime
My achievements and my failures,
Tell me that there are no saviors.
I'm not sure, what I'm handing on
Really there is just one thought
I will allow
It's not about pleasure or even treasure
But a point of view that I will avow
Never more than now.

NO REGRETS

She looked at him and squeezed his hand
She said to him "I miss you and
"I miss the person that I am
When I'm with you."
He looked around the room and sighed
And thought "She's so self-satisfied
"There's a hundred I could have outside
If I wanted to."

You can stay,
Or you can walk away
There's nothing they can do,
There's nothing they can say.

They stood there waiting for the train
Explanations made in vain
She tossed her head in plain disdain
And made no reply.
He waited for the ice to thaw
He knew he'd said it all before
He wondered if he was a bore,
Then he made another try.

You can stay,
Or you can walk away
There's nothing they can do,
There's nothing they can say.
No regrets, it's as good as it gets
No regrets at all.

You see that time is nature's way
Of separating yesterday
From tomorrow and today
So there's no disarray.
So what has happened up to now
Doesn't matter anyhow
Go on, take a nice deep bow
And resume the passion play.

You can stay,
Or you can walk away
There's nothing they can do,
There's nothing they can say.
No regrets, it's as good as it gets
No regrets at all.

NOTHING IS ALLOWED

Nothing is allowed
Everything is possible ...

I'll tell you 'bout China
Land of Confucius and Mao
Which one to praise and blame?
Both get to take a bow.

No guilt, just shame
if you're caught in the act
You're a friend you're fine
A stranger's fair game, that's a fact.

Nothing is allowed
Everything is possible ...

I'll fill you in on
The Hu, the Hao and the Wen
They've got their own way
Lenin laced with zen

Everything is black and white
In the USA
In China, that's not right
Everything is grey

Nothing is allowed
Everything is possible ...

Contradictions co-exist
Have done for five thousand years
Legalese and logic? Western
Wetness behind the ears

The system is genius,
The genius of the grey
Everything's so flexible
Communism in Cathay.

NUMBER ONE

There's just no doubt about it
I'm gonna have to shout it out
I can do it, I know that I can do it
I just found out, there's really nothing to it.
I can feel the power
It's growing by the hour now
Oh, I'm in it to win it
I'm not here to lose.

   Number one, I'm gonna try for
   Number one, No one could ask more
   Number one, I'm gonna outscore
   Everybody, I'm heading for the top floor.

How am I expected
To keep my feet down on the ground
Every little thing is going my way
This winning streak I'm on is here to stay.
All my dreams can come true
I'm Wellington at Waterloo
The only limits left
Are those that I choose.

   Fear of flying is for the future
   I will be what I want to be
   Fear of dying is for those who are older
   Those whose hearts are colder
   I've got immortality.

   Chorus

Every day's my birthday
Every day there's something new
Show me a hill,
I'll find a way to climb it
Show me a rhyme,
I'll find a way to rhyme it.
I've got to seize the moment
I know that it was heaven sent
There's an offer here
That I cannot refuse.

   Chorus

OH HUGO

A song written on the day my grandson was born

I see a ladder stretching up and down
Lost in the clouds and down on the ground
Those on the upper rungs
Are no longer very clear
But there's someone new, on the first rung
Hugo is here.

   Oh Hugo,
   Welcome to the world
   Oh Hugo,
   With your fingers soft and curled

Eyes and toes, ears and nose,
All present and correct
As good a start as anyone
Ever could expect.
So sleep a while,
It's all in front of you
All that you'll become,
And all that you will do.

Oh Hugo,
Welcome to the world
Oh Hugo,
With your fingers soft and curled
Oh Hugo,
We wish you health and smiles
Success and wealth if possible,
And not too many trials.

   Oh Hugo

ONE FALSE MOVE

One false move and you're history
Nothing you can do, no turning back
Ain't no doubt, there's no mystery
You'll never get a second crack.

   Bad day, wrong way,
   You know who is going to pay
   Don't expect no sympathy
   Who me you'll see,
   Condemnation comes for free
   You can depend upon your friends
   To send some roses to the cemetary.

It isn't paranoia
Cos it isn't hard to prove
There's a line of people
With daggers in their hands
Waiting for my first false move.

   Chorus

One little slip 'twixt the cup and the lip
Will leave your prospects in the dirt
It's all very fine to cry over split wine
But the stain on your character
Will match that on your shirt.

   Chorus

ONE LITTLE MILLION

All I want is one little million
One little million, just one million
All I want is one little million
Then I'll be okay.

All I want is one little million
One little million, just one million
All I want is one little million
Then I'm on my way.

What can I say…
Actually no way.

All I want is two little million
Two little million, just two million
All I want is two little million
Then I'm be satisfied.

All I want is two little million
Two little million, just two million
All I want is two little million
Then I'm on the right side.

I lied,
Okay I lied.

All I want is three little million
Three little million, just three million
All I want is three little million
That would be enough.

All I want is three little million
Three little million, just three million
All I want is three little million
That would be perfectly sufficient.

For a while
It'll tide me over
Tide me over …

Three may be too optimistic
Two may still be somewhat tight
But let's not be pessimistic
One will be … just alright.

I'll put up with one little million
One little million, just one million
I'll put up with one little million
That's enough for me.

I'll put up with one little million
One little million, just one million
I'll put up with one little million
Preferably tax-free.

ONE MORE DAY

Once in a while
In a conversation
Over dinner with a friend
I espy in their words
A puzzling and premature
Assumption of an end.

Another ten years
That'd surely be enough
Don't want to be here
When the rest of them
Have all passed on.
My dog just died,
Don't intend to get another
No one to look out for him
When I am gone.

   I'm sitting here in the sun
   Wondering whose will is done
   By second guessing movements
   Of the hand of fate
   Restrictions and reductions
   Redactions and deductions
   You change your mind
   You might find it's too late.

Damned if you don't,
And damned if you do, you say
But can't isn't won't
There's no replay
But answer me
If you knew it was tomorrow
Would you ask for one more day.

   One more day for the world,
   To delight 'em
   And one more day after that,
   Ad infinitum.

All that I know
If asked the same question
Is that I hope I'd reply
I aim for the most
And never to coast
To be alive the day I die.

OUT OF THE BLUE

I was flying from Manila to Hong Kong and looked of the window. This is what I saw in the clouds.

I saw a giant standing tall and lonely
Watching as the silver bird flew by
A sleeping man was lying on the dark sea
A trickle of ink ran from his eye.

I saw a wise king with his crown and sceptre
Gazing out across the eastern sea
A woman with hair piled high above her
Pointed at a little cat, perched up in a tree.

Clouds in a collisseum
Actors and actresses, moving on cue
Nobody else can see them
Come out of the blue.

A teddy bear with tumours fat and furry
Sitting in a chariot pulled by whales
Raised his paw and told them all to hurry
Cross the carpet of tortoises and snails.

A sphinx with a line of Mayan statues
A Buddha with a radio-active heart
Fred Flintstone, Fred Flintstone
With is hands on his knees
Blowing on a tanker to push it off the chart.

    Clouds in a collisseum
    Actors and actresses, moving on cue
    Nobody else can see them
    Come out of the blue.

The dinosaur was laughing at the tortoise
While Sherlock Holmes
Reclined upon the floor
A beggar with a veil of mist
Around his face
Reached out to grab the silver bird
Before it reached the shore.

    Clouds in a collisseum
    Actors and actresses, moving on cue
    Nobody else can see them
    Come out of the blue.

OUT ON THE ROAD

I've been walking
Hiding out on the road
I've been talking
To everyone out on the road.
I don't know what's round the next corner
There's no signs or binary code
I just take it
The way it goes out on the road.

I've been thinking
Weighing things out on the road
I've been shrinking
With every step out on the road.
I know what I'm leaving behind me
I'm shrugging off my special load
No regrets as
I make my way out on the road

I'll keep walking
I see no reason to end
I'll keep talking,
And wondering what's there round the bend
We all have a million choices
Nothing is given or owed
I'm just glad that
I'm walking here out on the road.

OVER THE RIDGE

There was a day in 2006 when I was walking beyond the town of Yuexi in southwest Anhui, up and up into the mountains, and when I crossed one particular ridge it was a transcendental moment. The sense of two separate worlds, one on each side of the ridge. These words don't do justice to the moment.

I walked up and up
The mountain road steep and winding
 Daring me to give in

The ridge was above me
And above it only the sky

I puffed on
The cicadas screamed in delight

I wiped me brow
I saw the ridge ahead
I felt a breeze
And I walked through the gap
Into a new world

Over the ridge
Into a new world
Over the ridge
Into a new place
Over the ridge
Into a new life
Over the ridge
Into a new space
Over the ridge
Into a new world

Changes, changes, changes, changes
A change in the atmosphere
A change in the air
It's all more clear
I'm more aware
A change in perspective
There's hope there in the sky

A change in the way I live
An answer to the question why
I can change
I know I can change.

PANIC EARLY

> This song, and parts of several others, was inspired by my great friend and guide through so much of my life and around many twists and turns, Gareth Powell. A basic rule of life, he said, is that if you're going to panic, panic early. I linked it here to the financial markets because I was working at the time (the late 1980s) at Reuters news agency, covering the collapse of the markets following Black Friday in 1987.

It's up, it's down,
It's going round and round
The greed and the panic,
Gonna nail us to the ground.
We're trapped inside,
The whole world's going broke
They call it economics,
But it looks more like a joke.

At times like this,
It's better to be poor
Cos you don't miss money
That you've never had before
The numbers change,
Sometimes fast and sometimes slow
But when the prices fall,
Where does all the money go?

Don't listen to the gurus,
They'll put you in the deep, deep red
Here's the only advice,
That might help you stay ahead:
If you're gonna panic, panic early.
If you're gonna panic, panic early.

You place your bets
Then you close your eyes and pray
That the numbers of the green screens
Decide to go your way
Black Monday and Tuesday,
Wednesday and Thursday
Will make Black Friday
Seem a charming shade of grey.

Now the man who said
What goes up must go back down
Is proven every day
To be much more than just a clown
I sell at the low,
I purchase at the high
I'd sell the whole damn lot
Except I don't know what to buy.

Don't listen to the gurus,
They'll put you in the deep, deep red
Here's the only advice,
That might help you stay ahead:
If you're gonna panic, panic early.

PEKING ALL-STARS

I ran the best rock band in China for four years in the early 1980s. I know it was the best because it was the only rock band in China. I was the singer and rhythm guitarist, but more importantly I owned the drums and the amps. The band members changed over the years, but they were all foreigners. A young Chinese trumpet player named Cui Jian wanted to join the band at one point, but I turned him down because I thought it would hurt his career prospects if he was to associate with foreigners.

We are the Peking All-Stars,
The best damn band in town
We are the Peking All-Stars,
The best damn band in town
When it comes to rock and roll,
We're the only ones around.

We're waiting to be discovered,
By the chinese people's record company
We're waiting to be discovered,
By the chinese people's record company
We'll fly into the hit parade
And make it straight to number Yi.

We'll party with the party
And disco 'til we drop
It would take a party congress
To ever make us stop
We are the Peking All-Stars
The best damn band in town
When it comes to rock and roll,
We're the only ones around.

We's playing for de peoples
Just every chance we get
We's playing for de peoples
Just every chance we get
We socialise so much
We may become socialist yet.

We're aiming for the big time
And we just don't think it's fair
We're aiming for the big time
And we just don't think it's fair
That they won't let us play
Down there in Tian An Men Square.

Chorus

RACING

This was my life for most of the 2010s

I'm racing to the airport
Running for the train
Vying for a taxi
Adrenaline controls my brain.

A mighty multi-tasker
I crave complexity
To do list at the ready
Don't have a smart phone, I've got three.

   I'm racing around the world
   I'm racing around the world
   I'm racing around the world
   Watch out, I'm coming through.

I have no time for downtime
I'm always power on
A glimpse of passing flowers
They're here and then … they're gone.

I measure out the madness
In meetings, mails and calls
It's been this way for years
I got no time for trips … or falls.

   I'm racing around the world
   I'm racing around the world
   I'm racing around the world
   Watch out, I'm coming through.

Should I sit beneath a tree,
And drift away
What's the point of racing
Racing racing, every day
People say let time slow right down,
Through plain inaction
I've thought about it,
Considered it and mulled it,
There's only one reaction:

I'm racing

I guess I'll keep running
Movement feels okay
Let's assume it's progress
As I run away.

REAL CITY HEROES

The inspiration for this was a series of youtube videos for kids in which the cars talk to each other. But I think that's what we need – some real city heroes. By which I don't mean vigilantes, but rather people who take a principled stand on what is happening around them.

Too positive, it's often said
But that's the sound inside my head
I wouldn't want you to be misled
It's true, these are desperate days

Now you and I, we've walked the stage,
Perspective comes to those of age
Not to mention fear and rage
Watching as the world decays.

We need ...

Real City Heroes
To chip away, to face the slime
One smile at a time
Real City Heroes
They balance out each awful crime
Match the vicious and vile
With sublime.

Happiness is a butterfly
Try to catch it, before you die
Start by working on those nearby
What do you have to lose?

Wake up every morning
And treat everybody right
Try to do more good than bad
Don't be black, be white - in moral terms

   Human nature is good not evil
   Call me naive, but I believe
   Human nature is good not evil
   Call me naive, but I believe in

Real City Heroes
To chip away, to face the slime
One smile at a time
Real City Heroes
They balance out each awful crime
Match the vicious and vile
With sublime.

REALLY REALLY REALLY

I feel so down I wanna die
I got nothing left to lose
I feel so down I wanna die
Especially when I watch the news
But that's only on a good day
You should see me when I
Really, really, really
Got the blues.

Well, my baby's gone and left me
And I'm left alone and cryin'
Yeah, my baby's gone and left me
And I done gone broke my spine
Oh I'd say my situation
Frankly speaking is
Really, really, really
Less than fine.

I can do other colours too,
I'm not limited to blue
I may be white but that's okay,
I like my music any way but grey
Black humor and purple prose,
Pink romance, I got all of those
Here's my hand,
And here's my plectrum,
Watch it race right up the spectrum.

I got Prussian, I got navies
In deep and garish hues
I got peacocks, ducks and babies
Shades both subtle and obtuse
I got sapphire, steel and aqua
Of all the colours I have
Really, really, really
Got the blues.

RESPECT (IT IS WHAT IT IS)

The starting point for this song was the Chinese phrase *meibanfa* "没辦法", which roughly means "there's nothing that can be done about it." It's the curse of China. But generally speaking, I don't think anything is inevitable unless you decide it is.

Let me describe the scene of the crime
Give a sense of what we have become
From aspiring to climb
To the state of sublime
We are now just uncomfortably numb

Together alone, the moments drift by
We click and we swipe and we stream
What we were, what we are,
And what we will be
All bundled up inside a dream.

It is what it is

Maybe I'm passive, maybe tuned out
I prefer to play dumb most the time
Faced with the scale,
Like a fish to a whale
Complicity is my own, it's my own crime.

My brain, in a bid to stay sane
Decided to split and lay low
The layer on top
Is all knee-jerk acceptance
The layer below's where I know.

It is what it is ... that's what they say
I prefer to believe there's a way
I say no no no no
It's not necessarily, necessarily so
No No No
I know the circumstance, what to expect
What I really require
Is just basic respect.

Where is it going, what does it mean?
How does it link the past?
Above and below,
Beyond and between
There's a void in the place of what's past.

You can say things are better,
The challenges less
We nod and we think nothing deep
Anonymous nobodies,
Nothing unless
We decline to be lulled into sleep.

It is what it is ... that's what they say
I prefer to believe there's a way
I say no no no no
It's not necessarily,
Necessarily so
No No No
This may be trickier than you suspect
So much forgotten,
Twisted and wrecked
Yes, I know the circumstance,
What to expect
But there's hope of another way,
One of respect.

ROOM WITH A VIEW

I want a room with a view in it
I want a room with a view of you
No need for windows or TV in it
A view of only you would do

It doesn't have to be luxurious
It can be ugly, and spartan too
I'm not particularly curious
Just want a room with a view of you.

    I want a room with a view
    Not of the sky so blue
    I want a room with a view
    Not of a sea of bamboo
    I want a room with a view
    Not of Xanadu
    I want a room with a view
    Of you.

Not of the mountains in Peru
Not of the subject most taboo
Not of a beach near Cebu
Not of a blue kazoo in kalamazoo.

I want a room with a view in it
I want a room with a view of you
I don't CARE what ELSE there IS in it
There's nothing THAT could improve on you.

I need a room with a view in it
I want that room that contains just we two
No need to even have a light in it
I can use my haaaands, to feel the view

    I want a room with a view
    Not of Katmandu
    I want a room with a view
    Not of the sun shining through
    I want a room with a view
    Not of Timbuktu
    I want a room with a view
    Of you.

SAKE O SAKE

For many years I had dinner in a Japanese restaurant every day, eating salmon sashimi and cucumber sticks and drinking warm sake. This song was inspired by that experience.

I was sitting at the counter
Of a Japanese restaurant,
Drinking rice wine, that's sake,
It was piping hot
All alone in that restaurant,
People swirling around me,
The sake really hit the spot
It was Asian and aromatic,
I thought, you know,
This drink is just about everything I'm not.

So I had another bottle,
Savoring the flavor,
As a guy came to the counter,
Sat down right next to me.
He also ordered sake,
I looked at him,
And he looked at me
i toasted him, I said "the sake twins",
He said it looks like it was meant to be.

We sat there getting sozzled,
Talked 'bout life and business,
The good and the bad,
The known and the unknown
About investing money
Making money losing money,
Thile the PA played some jazz
With a saxophone
The guy said this sake's grand,
Why don't we make our own brand,
Sell it on out own?

For sure a success,
He said a shoe-in more or less
We'll make money in wads
We just need a name,
I said that's my game
"Why don't we call it "for god's"

Sake o sake, for god's sake
Sake o sake, for god's sake
Sake o sake o sake o sake, for god's sake.

He said that joke's pretty weak,
But who am I to critique,
I don't want to seem like a pain in the neck
I said: I think so too,
But it's the best that I can do,
After all this sake, what the heck

He said Fair enough oh!
Look at the time, it's time to go!
He stood up, walked out the door
And left me with the check.

Sake o sake, for god's sake
Sake o sake, for god's sake
Sake o sake o sake o sake,
For god's sake.

SATELLITE

The satellites are sailing
Slowly cross the sky
I wonder who they're talking to
Signals spinning through the night
Climbing half way to the moon
(On a summer's night)

Dishes gazing quietly into outer space
I wonder who they're listening to
Like flowers to the sun
Like disciples to the One

   We turn our eyes to heaven
   We take what we are given
   From the skies above
   It's nothing to do,
   It's nothing to do with love
   We sit our minds wide open
   Accept the future hoping
   That it's clear and bright
   Satellite.

A daisy chain of beacons
Laced around the world
A few more stars to light the way
I'm standing down below
In an electronic glow
(On a summer's night)

Flocks of feathered modems
Flying overhead
They've had their day, they've been retired,
The bigger birds have won
Flying closer to the sun
Chorus

Oh they control the telephones,
And they control the screens
This isn't how we planned it,
The plan isn't ours it seems
Oh they control the battlegrounds,
A myriad machines
When will they, Oh, when will they,
Control our dreams?

Chorus

SOCIALISM

I thought this was Red China
But the colors seem to fade away
Truth be said, it doesn't look so red
I'd say it's much more gray.

Tell me what happened to China
I must confess that I'm confused
Tell me what happened to China
I got those Marx and Lenin,
Mao Zedong Blues

    Communistic millionaires
    It sounds a little strange
    When the road to revolution
    Leads right through the stock exchange.

All the sharks invoke Karl Marx
It's better to be red than dead
But then again, they're all smart men
They know it's even better to be rich
instead.

Communistic millionaires
It sounds a little strange
When the road to revolution
Leads right through the stock exchange

Yes I thought this was Communist China
But it's looking much more fun
There's certainly no socialism finer
And the party's just begun

thanks to
Socialism with Chinese characteristics
Socialism with Chinese characteristics

STATUS QUO

A muse on a political system

We asked you here, to make it clear
Ensure that you would let you know
The job for you, is simply to
Maintain the status quo.

    Maintain, maintain,
    Maintain the status quo.
    Maintain, maintain,
    Maintain the status quo.

The means to use, are yours to choose
Reap only what we sow
Do what it takes, make no mistakes
Don't lose the status quo.

    Maintain, maintain,
    Maintain the status quo.
    Maintain, maintain,
    Maintain the status quo.

They say
The end justifies the means
They say
The world belongs to your son and mine
They say
Keep reality behind the screens
They say
Do what you like, but hold the line.

The time's at hand, you'll make a stand
But if it fails, we'll go
The cash is gone, the passport? Done
We'll leave the status quo.

    Maintain, maintain,
    Maintain the status quo.
    Maintain, maintain,
    Maintain the status quo.

STOMACH ACID

Hi, I'm a stomach acid,
My job is mashing up your food
I masticate it, disintegrate it,
Making sure it's good and chewed.

The name is Hydrochloric,
Food digestion section seven
We have a 3-shift system down here,
I'm on from 4 to 11 ... the dinner shift.

    I said hi, hi, hydrochloric,
    I love to get my teeth in some steak
    Hi, hi hydrochloric,
    Now roll on the next meal break.

One day while off duty,
I got a call on my bleeper to say
The taste buds had reported
A red pepper heading our way.

"Action stations fellas,
Catch him or he'll go straight on through!"
So we tied him down,
We cooled him down,
And we pulversed that pepper
Good and true.

    Chorus

In the mornings I'm on training,
Teaching little acids their trade
Any acid that can mash
A pound of peanuts in a flash
I would say had already made the grade.

Sometimes the little acids ask me
What it is their work is meant to be
I wait a while, then smile a smile
And say it's ... alimentary.

    Chorus

SUNSHINE

Sunshine, sunshine
Gold and bold and never far away
Sunshine, sunshine
Tell me if you're coming out today.

It was cloudy all day yesterday,
It rained the day before
I haven't seen you for so long
There ought to be a law
To keep the weather well-behaved
And every morning fine
Afternoons and evenings too
Now come on toe the line, sunshine.

Sunshine, sunshine
Gold and bold and never far away
Sunshine, sunshine
Tell me if you're coming out today.

I think you ought to show yourself
It's really time you did
Just throw away those big black clouds
Behind which you've been hid
It's almost time for breakfast
The clock says ten to nine
If you could use a knife and fork
I'd ask you out to dine, sunshine.

Sunshine, sunshine
Gold and bold and never far away
Sunshine, sunshine
Tell me if you're coming out today.

TAKE NOTHING

This is a lyric written for a tune on an environmentally friendly album called I Care sold through Body Shop outlets in Hong Kong in the early 1990s.

From the treetops,
Down through the heat
Past the marching armies
Of the forest floor
Hear the sentry upon his beat
Calling out to those
Who pass through Nature's door.

   Listen to me listen,
   All who come please listen
   Listen to me listen,
   We need your help please listen

In the twilight of dappled green
Far below the tangled canopy I stand
Up above me, the sentry sings
In a language all of us can understand.

Listen to me listen,
All who come please listen
Listen to me listen,
We need you help
Please listen

Take nothing, take nothing,
But your memories
Leave nothing, leave nothing,
But your dreams
Take nothing, take nothing,
You can't see the forest
If you take the trees
Leave nothing, leave nothing,
But footprints in the streams.
It may not seem to matter,
But nothing's as it seems.

Listen to me listen,
All who come please listen
Listen to me listen,
We need your help please listen

Take nothing, take nothing,
But your memories
Leave nothing, leave nothing,
But your dreams
Take nothing, take nothing,
You can't see the forest
If you take the trees
Leave nothing, leave nothing,
But footprints in the streams.
It may not seem to matter,
But nothing's as it seems.

It may not seem to matter,
It seems so strong
It may not seem to matter,
But it won't last long
It may not seem to matter,
But nothing's as it seems.

TAO PARTY

This lyric attempts to summarize the basic tenets of Taoism. If I was to choose to believe in a religion, it would be this one.

The Tao is mischievous
The Tao is mysterious
The Tao's a paradox
The Tao knocks off your socks
The Tao is nothing and everything,
All at the same time.

The Tao, the more you have
The Tao, the less you got
The Tao, the more you are
The Tao, the more you're not
Laozi's laughing, and everything
Tends to the mean.

   Tao Party,
   The Tao that can't be named
   Tao Party,
   The Tao that can't be tamed

All hail duality
Black and white, all colors be
Close your eyes to see the light
Strength loses, weakness is might
The Tao rules but makes
No sense,
No sense at all.

Decay precedes re-birth
Success ain't what you think it's worth
Everything reverts to zero
Perceived failure makes you into a hero
Cycles cycles cycles cycles cycles cycles

Tao Party, the Tao that can't be named
Tao Party, the Tao that can't be framed
Tao Party, it's not a religion
Tao Party, it's more like a vision
Without circumcision

All ends are just a start
The Tao is at the heart
The reduction of Heaven and Earth,
The reversion of Death and Birth
Chaos is order and order is chaos,
And God is irrelevant.

You think you know? you're wrong
You think you don't? you're strong
You yield? That's no mistake
You don't, you could well break
The paradoxes rule,
Don't get too smart, you fool.

Tao Party, the Tao that can't be named
Tao Party, it can't be followed,
Tamed or framed
Tao Party, the Tao is beyond all ken
Tao Party, of course beyond all Zen
Tao Party, more basic than Higgs-Boson
Tao Party, the Tao is the one,
The Tao is the chosen ...

THE ALIEN

The alien landed,
The planet was shocked
Crowds gathered round,
Near the place the ship docked.
The spaceship door opened,
The alien stepped out
The crowd looked in horror
And started to shout.

   "It's a monster we're finished,
A beast of this kind
Can only have come
With destruction in mind"
"Oh," they all thought,
As they looked at his face
"I'm glad I was born as I am,
And not of his race."

The alien too
Was most shocked at the sight
Of the strange beings crowded
Around him so tight.
He blinked both his eyes
And he scratched at his nose
He thought to himself,
I've seen nothing like those.

   "Their skin is bright orange,
Their head is a claw
And I've never seen beings
With ten eyes before."
"Oh," thought the alien,
"I'm glad that my birth
Was not on this planet
But on dear Mother Earth."

TALKIN' HONG KONG
(WITH APOLOGIES TO BOB DYLAN)

I remember the night
The plane touched down
And I found myself in Hongkong town
Stunned by the lights
And the smells and the sights
Didn't sleep at all that very first night
Wall-to-wall Chinese,
Money come out of their mouths.

Wintertime in Hongkong Town
The wind blows the garbage round
Took a trip to Kowloonside
Star Ferry cost just ten cents a ride
Bit more expensive now,
But then you get silver seats to slide on.

Spent a lot of time just ramblin' round
Finding out about ol' Hongkong Town
Went to Temple Street and Cat Street too
Saw everything and it all was new
Looking at the faces,
Lusting after the young female bodies.

Learned to use chopsticks, rode on a tram
Found out that Maxim's is a sham
Read the Standard the Star
And the Morning Post
Couldn't work out
Which I loathed the most
If it wasn't for Frank & Earnest,
Wizard of Id and Dear Pansy
I would've stopped reading newspapers
A long time ago.

Found myself a job and a place to stay
Got set up in a pretty good way
I guess I had my ups and downs
But I finally fell in love
With Hongkong Town

Oh I know it's dirty and ugly and crowded
... taxi drivers are rude ... nowhere to go
on Sundays ...   too hot in summer, too cold
in winter ...   never any good movies ...
you can never find a fake Rolex when you
want one ...   ... you have to spend your
life avoiding conversations about 1997 ....
BUT IT'S NOT BORING.

THAT'S MY NUMBER

This really is my mobile number, You will be required at the end of the song to tell me my phone number.

I have a phone, a smart phone
Smarter than me, but it's mine alone
It has a number, the number's mine
The number's me, that's the bottom line.

   139 016 68748

The number's tattooed on my brain
Not on my wrist, still in the public domain
You call it, you got me
I'm there, faster than a s a p

   139 016 68748

The phone is here, my link to god
A filter and a lightning rod
It rules my life, it works a dream.
It gives me news and ... self-esteem

   139 016 68748

Ignore the magnetic emissions
Just make more online decisions
Call them call you call me out loud
Photograph your soul,
Transmit it to the cloud

   139 016 68748
   That's my number
   That's my number
   That's my number
   That's my number

THE BEANS

There's a Taoism element to this lyric.

What do you mean, there's no more coffee
Do I have to do it all
What is the point, no I don't drink tea
Whatever happened
To your famous total recall.

I have this image of you lying there
And nothing getting done
No, please don't tell me that I'm right
That would simply spoil the fun.

   It's not about the beans
   You're right about that
   You're just venting
   You've got you're line down pat

You chose a bad day,
To pull this kind of trick
We've discussed this all before
What amazes me is how it doesn't stick
I must have told you
A thousand times or more.

It drives me crazy, the coffee's typical
Why not be in control
Make lists, don't forget, do it now
These are the virtues that you know I extol.

   It's not about the beans
   You're right about that
   You're just venting, only venting
   You've got you're line down pat

Wu wei, No way
Wu wei, Anyway
Wu wei, What can I say
Wu wei, Okay
Wu wei, Your way
Wu wei, Anyway
Wu wei, What can I say
Wu wei, But okay.

I concede sometimes I'm too intense
My patience wears thin fast
There's no doubt that I'm over-stressed
But I really want this last.

You should have learned by now,
This is a phase
I need to get it off my chest
The coffee's still problem, but yes I agree
Let's put it aside, get on with the rest.

   It's not about the beans
   You're right about that
   You're just venting, simply venting
   You've got you're line down pat

THE DEAL IS ON

I'm working on a deal
With big potential
Here's the business plan
It's confidential

I can bring you in, I can make your day
We can work it out, sign this NDA
The deal I'm working on
Has big potential.

The terms I'm offering you
Are preferential
Just calculate
The differential

I can bring you in, I can make your day
We can work it out, sign this NDA
The deal I'm working on
Has big potential.

And when we list on a stock exchange
I'm not sure which
We'll price the shares at a premium
And we'll be rich, yes rich, I tell you rich …

The profit growth will be
Exponential (believe you me)
No no, there's no need to be
So deferential (see the ppt)

But I can bring you in, I can make your day
We can work it out, sign this NDA
The deal I'm working on
Has big potential.

THE LAST PANDA

This is a reworking of the song The Sky, imagining the last panda in the wild.

There at the edge of the world
She stood alone with her eyes on us all
She swayed side to side in the darkness
As she calmly awaited the call.

For months she had wandered about
Growing older and slower and blind
In her bones she had known
For some time now
That she was the last of her kind.

    The Sky, The Sky

Caught between nature and man
In a vice that she couldn't escape
The bamboo was dying around her
The forest, a victim of rape.

Her home was no longer her home
Invaded by giants in herds
They crashed through
The forest around her
And gathered to look at her turds.

The Sky, will be your home tonight
The Sky, will make you feather light
Everything must end,
No reason to weep
It is not your fault now
Lay down to sleep.

   The Sky, Sky

Once on a hill far away
As she sat munching leaves in the shade
Her children rolled round in the sunshine
Beating down from a sea of blue jade.

Gone are the sun and the dreams
Gone as well are the children she bore
Either dead or else clowns in a circus
It didn't matter any more.

THE MEMORY STAYS

A song marking the death of my mother

Remember the time,
How could I forget it
The time was so fine,
Nothing could upset it
The days were so bright,
Everything was crystal clear
And the nights,
When the stars all seemed so near.

Remember the place,
Close my eyes I'll be there
The smile on my face,
Tells you what I see there

Nothing has changed,
Behind the veil it's all the same
All arranged,
And awaiting memory's flame.

Mark the years off in my diary
Watch the colours turning to grey
The people I used to know
Have all gone their own ways
But no matter at all
I know that the memory stays.

Remember the one,
No, it doesn't grieve me
It's not all gone,
The memory won't leave me
Time to turn round,
And make tomorrow yesterday
Oh I'm bound,
To salt more memories away.

Mark the years off in my diary
Watch the colours turning to grey
The people I used to know
Have gone their own separate ways
But no matter at all
I know that the memory stays.
The memory stays, the memory stays ....

THE MOTIVE

A song about surveillance, a conversation between Big Brother and a bewildered ordinary person

I am sending a message,
No recipient named
It's just for you
About online surveillance
And at whom it is aimed
What is your view?

The easy assumption is surveillance is evil
But I'm not sure
Anonymous trawling for data retrieval
Feels less than pure.

   Your message is received,
   We're glad you asked
   This impacts on the way we live
   But the issue isn't monitoring,
   Oh no
   It's all about the motive.

The motive, that's what I'm thinking
Where does this go
I see a black hole, I feel we are sinking
But what would I know.

And hey, what's the deal
In Beijing and Caracas
Things there seem less than fine
Is it more nefarious or just like us
Big Brother of mine?

   You make a valid point, there are places
   Where things are not so easy to forgive
   Our view is there are differences

Our advice is to focus on the motive.

If it's about the motive, then show me
How to tell good from bad
With the benefit of ignorance behind me
This is driving me mad.

All I want is protection
Now that privacy's gone
Never alone, but always lonely
From now on.

If you were making a movie
On the end of the world
Why not start here
An impossible problem
The future unfurled
A future I fear.

There's no need to be glum,
It's not that bad
The chances are nobody cares
What you have to give.
But surveillance now is for all time
Just figure out the motive.

THE PCH
(PACIFIC COAST HIGHWAY)

I'm on my way
They say dreams can come true
The sky's as wide as the future
The road, it runs right through.
The Pacific Coast Highway
Heading for LA
This is the one, this is the chance
I'll beat them all, and I'll break away.

I own this road
Every inch is mine
A one lane highway on my side
Part of a grand design.

Cliffs bear down upon me
Rollers lead me astray
But I'll find a way between them all
I'll make my own path and I'll break away.

San Francisco and Pescadero
Monterey and Carmel
Big Sur and Morro Bay
Paso Robles and Pismo Beach
Arroyo Grande and Vandenberg
Santa Ynez and Santa Barbara
Ventura, Malibu
Santa Monica and Century City

Inspiration
These places have it all
Big Sur is still Big Sur
Even when traffic's at a crawl.
The pounding Pacific
The air like sweet sorbet
The bling's ahead, you heard what i said
This is it now, all the way.

North to south
The sun is in my eyes
The ocean's deep and oh so wide
With all that that implies.
It's one of those days
When the world's much more than okay
The change is on, my doubts are gone,
I'll beat them all, I'm gonna break away…

THE PRIORITIES

This was written in honor of my sister's husband. An excellent fellow.

There once was a young fella named Cary
With absolutely no intention to marry
His life was most happy, at sea or the bar,
Fishing was his passion, his favorite by far.

But then – oh no! A calamity occurred,
A development so dire
He was lost for a word
Old age raised its head, in a tentative way
He felt his mortality grow by the day.

   Oh, the priorities
   We line them all up every day
   Decide what you want
   Make each choice yay or nay
   Work out what's a go
   And what's really no way

Casting about for a solution to his woes
He said "I know!
A pretty girl will keep me on my toes".
Fishing was stopped
And drinking curtailed,
All energies spent searching
Until he prevailed.

Along came a beauty - sensual and hot,
He said to himself
"Wow; she's everything I'm not"
Small, slim, fast-talker,
A damn good cook too,
He said: "She's fantastic,
She'll jolly well do".

Oh, the priorities
We line them all up every day
Decide what you want
Make each choice yay or nay
Work out what's a go
And what's really no way

He plucked up his courage and said
"What's your name?"
Karen, she said,
And things were never the same.
That was years ago, today is today
He was back drinking and fishing, with but a little delay.

Karen tried hard
To keep her man on an even keel,
She even made changes
On the good ship Seal.
Like replacing all the beer
With bottles of Chardonay
Cary said "Nice try darlin',
But really no way."

Oh, the priorities
We line them all up every day
Decide what you want
Make each choice yay or nay
Choices like swapping beer out
For sweet Chardonnay
Cary said: "Nice try darlin',
But really no way."
Yes, he said "Nice try honey,
But really no way."

THE ROAD IS HARD
(WITH APOLOGIES TO LI BAI)

A golden flask of clearest wine,
A jade plate stacked with food so fine
I stop in mid-bite, put down my cup
And look around, my thoughts pent-up.

The Yellow River's frozen hard,
The mountains - snowbound and barred
So I sit and while away my time
Waiting for a chance to shine.

The road is hard, the road is hard,
With many forks along the way
The road is hard, the road is hard,
Where am I now, so hard to say.

I believe there'll come a day
When the wind will push the waves away
When I'll hoist my sail into the sky
And sail the great seas wide and high.

THE SKY

> This song was inspired by the suicides of three young friends all within a short space of time. The lady was Christine, tormented by a desire to escape, while the subject of the second set of verses was a homosexual man caught in the wrong era. The third was … lets call him Mahommed. He wanted to resign from the organization to which he belonged, but they wouldn't let him.

There at the edge of the world
She stood alone with her eyes on the void
She was seeking the freedom of silence
Not the hyper-awareness of Freud.

The bonds of intensity cracked
The colours and pain fell away
The demons that hide in the abyss
They were whispering to her, they'd say:

    The Sky, The Sky

Wit and intelligence fail
In the face of a dark, hidden shame
As he chain-smoked his way through the evening
He decided to change his own name.

Humour most black was the mask
Behind were the demons at play
A million beers and a needle
Couldn't cajole them away.

The Sky ... will be your home tonight
The Sky ... will make you feather light
You only have to take one last leap
To your final haven, lay down to sleep.

The Sky, The Sky

The screams of a tortured guitar
Were the cries of a mind in despair
He said "You can't know what it feels like,
This is not something that I can share."

The demons had stolen his soul
Watched his sanity melting away
He knew that he had to destroy them
Had to silence their taunts come what may.

The Sky ....

TIME TO RHYME

Another online songwriting course submission. The other students seemed to enjoy them.

Time to rhyme
Make them perfect
Time to rhyme
A perfect rhyme is perfect
Time to rhyme
It's called perfect cos it's perfect
(Show some respect)

I spend a lot of time listening to the radio
I only like the songs with perfect rhyme
Other kinds of rhymes just give me vertigo
They're close to being a heinous crime.

I reckon rhymes that are imperfect
Reflect lyrical laziness
Out, damned linguistic disconnect
That's what Shakespeare would say,
But I digress.

I'm in favor of rhyming dictionaries
They're convenient and mostly free
Now that last rhyme
Was definitely subtractive
Not as good as it could have been

"Not as good as it could be"
Would be perfect
Why compromise even on one line
I believe in saying no
To every language disconnect
Every line should be a perfect rhyme.
Except for this one.

Am I being a little too literal
Should I show more rhyming flexibility
But It's a mental discipline after all
(To rhyme with literal)
That's the way I want all my songs to be.

Sting is brilliant, there is no doubt about it
I'm a fan and I will shout about it
But there's surely a touch of sloth
In rhyming words like cough and
Nabokov.

In terms of rhyming schemes, I go with
perfect all the way
I prefer a b a b to a b b a
In fact there's also nothing wrong
With using a a a a
I never liked Abba anyway.

As to family rhymes, I just say Mama mia
I am not at all impressed
I believe that precise is nice
Even though you think incest is best

Time to rhyme

Chorus

TOUGH WORLD

This song was inspired by a vast area of prison farms near the town of Shayang in the western part of the Hubei plain in central China

I'm just a little bit older
The nights are certainly colder
But I know to survive
I'm still glad I'm alive.

I fight and I try
If needs be I'll even lie
A smile is always best
But I don't rule out the rest.

   It's a tough world
   It's a tough world in which we live
   It's a tough world
   But better than the alternative

I walk where they say
They'll get me if I stray
We walk in twos and threes
On the wrong side of the trees.

   It's a tough world
   It's a tough world in which we live
   It's a tough world
   But better than the alternative

TRYING TO WRITE A SONG

This was a tune written as part of an online songwriting course. The guru, who we only saw in videos, was (and probably still is) Pat Pattison.

I wrote some lyrics on some paper,
then put it in a box
Put the box inside another box,
Then another box around that
I listened hard from the outside,
Nothing could I hear
I wonder if I really understood the point,
Pat

Then you told me straight up
to get inside the box
So in I stepped and down I sat
I expected to find
My six best friends there for me
But I'm alone,
Where did they go, Pat?

I'm trying to write a song,
I follow every rule
Try to be a good student,
In this global music school
I can't see my school mates,
There is no lecture hall
I don't seem to be making
Any progress at all.

You told us a story about a plain girl
She looked like something
Brought in by the cat
But on her wedding day, yes,
She wore a beautiful dress
But what was the point of that, Pat?

Chorus

Massive open online courses
New communities
I watch the videos, read all the blogs
I'm trying as hard as I can to please

    I'm trying to write a song,
    I follow every rule
    Try to be a good student,
    In this global music school
    I can't see my school mates,
    There is no lecture hall
    I don't seem to be making
    Any progress at all.

WAITING

I may be wrong, I may be right
It doesn't matter at this time of night
Demons just beyond the light
Just in sight.

Watch the moon falling from the sky
Wonder what and wonder why
Wonder if it's worth another try
By and by.

Another cup of lemon tea
Another trip around the world that's me
Trapped between what is
And what should be
Set me free.

Silence blanketing the world outside
An emptiness as broad as it is wide
Nowhere to run, nowhere to hide
If I tried.

Waiting, for the sun to rise
Waiting, for the early morning sun
to open up my eyes.

The end of night or start of day
It doesn't matter much either way
Life goes on come what may
Or so they say.

It's time to stop, it's time to sleep
Thinking in circles leads me
Down too deep
Worries piled up in a heap
Too high to leap.

    Waiting, for the sun to rise
    Waiting, for the early morning sun
    to open up my eyes.
    Waiting, for the sun to rise
    Waiting, for the early morning sun
    to open up my eyes.

WAS WHAT IT WAS

An effort to sum up my life.

I've seen the sun, I've seen the rain
I'm not so smart, but I'm not insane
I've stumbled through the changes
In the best way that I know.

I'm not the same, they're not to blame
Two separate worlds, a different game
To know too much deranges
As I know that I can show.

    Rolling back the years
    The hopes and the fears
    I did what I could
    Much less than I should
    I'll make no excuses
    It was what it was.

I've seen the calm, I've seen the storm
I'm not so strange, but I'm not the norm
I've lived along the edges
For as long as I can say.

They live their lives, they don't touch mine
They walk on by, no word or sign
But then I have my thoughts
I'm fine in my own way.

    Rolling back the years
    The hopes and the fears
    I did what I could
    Much less than I should
    I'll make no excuses
    It was what it was.

WALKING WEST

Another song inspired by my cross-China trek. The key was a namecard with my phone number on it which I handed out to everybody..

I'm walking west,
To send a sign
To take what's best,
And retrieve what's mine.
I'm walking west,
To prove it's true
That you are me,
And I am you.

I'm walking west,
Because it's there
And to testify,
And because I care.
I'm walking west,
Handing out a key
To unlock the world,
And all we can be.

It's all a test
From trough to crest
Before I'm laid to rest
I'm walking I'm walking
I'm walking west.
... To open wide
(To leave the rest) ... On the other side

I accept the test
Nothing but the best
Before I'm laid to rest I'm walking ...
I'm walking west.

I'm walking west,
To send a sign
To take what's best,
And retrieve what's mine.
I'm walking west,
To prove it's true
That you are me,
And I am you.

WE'RE ALL THE SAME

A song related to the general joy I experienced walking through the countryside on my cross-China walk, an adventure which last for years. And which I will one day resume.

I like sunshine,
I like rain
A mountain breeze,
Ripe grain
Smiling faces,
Country lanes
Verdant valleys,
Wide wide plains.

We're all the same
Life's a business,
Life's a game
There's nothing new,
No one to blame
We have a conscience,
We have a name
We're all so different,
We're all the same.

I like salmon,
Cucumber too
Sake to me baby, do
Steaming coffee,
Sushi bar
Indian nan desuka?

Chorus

Gentle laughter,
Honest eyes
Hellos with a smile,
Goodbyes
Body language,
An offered ride
The rain beating down outside.

WHAT LOCKDOWN?

This song was inspired by the amazing Shanghai lockdown of 2022, when people were confined to their apartments for ten weeks, and in some cases even more. The system had the right to do it. But having done it, it thereby lost the ability to do it again.

I can walk to the bathroom
I can go to the kitchen any time
I can lie right down in the bedroom
That is not a problem, it's not a crime.

I can move through different states of mind
I can ramble anywhere around the web
I can ride the shifting tides of time
The rise and then the ebb.

   Oh my mind is free to wander
   And it wanders more and more
   Yes my mind is free to wander
   As regulated by the law.

So just what is your problem?
What's the reason for this deep dismay?
Can't you see, for you and me,
It's an opportunity
To meditate,
Yes, meditate
Our lives away.

   Oh my mind is free to wander
   And it wanders more and more
   Yes my mind is free to wander
   As regulated by the law.

WORKS OF ART

Two beatiful girls having lunch
In a cool and secluded location
They're dressed to impress
And to add a competitive sense
Of romance To the conversation
There are looking so hot,
And you know that they know it
They both know there are men,
Who are looking at them,
But they woudn't show it.

    Hypnoptic, quixotic
    Untouchable or the perfect goal
    Exotic, erotic
    Will they heal your heart
    Or steal your soul?

Two debonair guys standing tall
By the bar
Where they're nursing their Glasses
They're very aware
That the girls that are There
Might be tempted to stare
At their gym-toned asses
There are looking so hot,
And it's clear that they know it
They both know there are girls
Who are looking for whirls
And they don't want to blow it.

Chorus

Calculated works of art
More of brain, and less of heart
Self-aware and full of poise
Extra special girls and boys

Chorus

YOGHURT AND HONEY

Yoghurt and honey
Smooth and sunny
Luxury laced on a spoon
A smooth combination
The resulting sensation
Is one to which
I'm not immune

A balm for the soul,
Its beyond all debate
The only concern is
I'm putting on weight
Yoghurt and honey
Smooth and sunny
Luxury laced on a spoon

Yoghurt and honey
It's kind of funny
I used to kind of hate both
But put them together
They're fine fresh or whether
They're hosting

Yoghurt is formed through
Fermentation
Bacteria breeding in slime
Honey is worse
Bee regurgitation
So how come the taste is sublime?

Yoghurt and honey
Even runny
Has a taste that sings like a tune
Protein is sweeter
When it's excreta
It's neater than moon, June and croon.

My immunity system
Is feeling the boost
Energy's up,
Let's just say I'm seduced
Yoghurt and honey
Smooth and sunny
Luxury laced on a spoon.

HAROLD, THE KAMIKAZE STRAWBERRY

Written in a park in Berlin, on Earthday April 22, 1990

My name is Harold,
My life is so merry,
I'm a ripening, succulent,
Blood-red strawberry
My brothers and sisters
And I live so well
We are tended and nurtured
By good farmer Bell.

> Oh we love him so much,
> He is so good to us
> He guards us and helps us
> Like no one else does
> He's selfless and kind
> And he tends us with care
> Farmer Bell is a saint
> With compassion to spare.

Good Farmer Bell
Was around us today
And I'm sure I distinctly
Did hear him say
That we strawberries soon
Would be ready to sell.
He will pick us and sell us!
Oh! cruel Farmer Bell!

> Oh we hate him so much,
> He is making us fat
> Just to kill us and sell us,
> No more than that!
> Our fate, we now find,
> Is that we will be eaten.
> But will we give in?
> No, we will not be beaten.

My name is Harold,
I am no fairy
I'm a desperate cold
Kamikaze strawberry.
I will have my revenge
On old Farmer Bell.
For this treacherous act,
I will send him to hell.

    Oh we hate him so much, we will do
    What we must
    To bring Farmer Bell
    To an end that is just.
    He deceived us,
    He doesn't love us at all
    He will sell us for money,
    Does that not appall?

But how can I kill him?
Farmer Bell is so huge
And I'm a petite
Little strawberry rouge
I could throw myself at him
When he comes around,
Put out his eye
And knock him to the ground.
Then we could block up his mouth
And his nose
Until he stopped breathing.
Oh, do you suppose
That would work? Maybe not.
I know what we need
A professional assassin
To handle the deed.

But we don't have the money,
The strawberries cried
Harold was silent.
And then he replied:
I know what I'll do.
I will eat pesticide
Until poison chemicals
Fill my inside
Then I will make Farmer Bell
Want to eat me.
I'll poison him dead.
He will not defeat me.

Oh we hate him, we hate him,
We hate Farmer Bell
We hate him much more
Than we can ever tell
He wants to kill us,
But we'll kill him first
From the moment he raised us,
His life has been cursed.

Here he comes now!
Farmer Bell, oh please stop!
Pick me and eat me!
I'm the best of the crop!
He's done it! He plucked me,
He's chewing me well!
Argghhh! There go the poisons
To kill Farmer Bell.

You killed him, oh Harold,
Kamikaze strawberry
You've sent a message
Which is clear, oh so very
Strawberry liberation
Rules okay
It's kill or be killed
On the farms of today.

AGNES & EDWINA, THE STAR-STRUCK APPLES

All was quiet in the shop,
The fruit were asleep.
The slumbering oranges
Piled in a heap.
The pineapples snored,
The tangerines dreamed
Of a far-away land
Where the sun always seemed
To be shininzg and warm.
It was cold where they lay
On the shelves near the door,
In the hours before day.

"Good morning!"
The radio suddenly cried.
"It's time to wake up,
The sun's shining outside.
"We've got some hot tunes
To brighten your day
"We've got oldies but goodies
And needless to say
"We'll also play lots
Of the latest sensations.

"Our music's so good it
Causes heart palpitations."

The fruit all woke up
To the musical beat
They stretched and they yawned
And some tapped their feet.
But two of the apples,
They listened in awe
They'd never heard anything
Like it before.
The drum beat was shaking them,
Melodies flew
Synthesisers and guitars,
And vocals too.
They both thought:
"I could sing better myself,
"A star I will be,
No more stuck on the shelf."

Let me introduce you:
Agnes and Edwina.
Agnes was red,

Edwina was greener.
They suddenly knew
What they wanted to be -
Pop music stars
'Cos alternatively
They had an extremely
Strong kind of a hunch
That they could soon end up
As somebody's lunch.
They started to sing
And to wiggle about
They'd have shaken their hips
If they'd had them, no doubt.
Agnes was certain
That she had it made
She shouted: "I'll top
The Top Ten Fruit Parade."
"No, it's me that will make it,"
Edwina declared.
"A place in the spotlight
Cannot be shared."
They started to argue,
And violence was used
You know how a girl apple
Hates to be bruised.

Now as it happened,
One shelf below
Was an entrepreneurial durian
Named Joe.
He had a good nose for fruit acts,
It was said.
Bananarama
And the Grapeful Dead
Were just two of the groups
He was said to have found.
He looked up and said:
"Hey girls, I like your sound!
"A couple of good looking apples like you
"Could go far if you really wanted to to do.
"We'll make you a duo,
You can sing harmony.
"I'll manage you
For a twenty-five per cent fee."

Edwina and Agnes both scowled wickedly.
A duo was not
What they wanted to be.
"I wll only sing solo,"
Said Agnes, and pouted.
"So will I, I won't sing with her,"
Edwina shouted.

"Now Cherry Lee Lewis,
He made it alone,"
Agnes added. "He had no need of a clone."
"And also Chuck Berry," Edwina replied.
"Mixed fruit salad was something
He could never abide."

"If you say so," said Durian Joe,
"But you see
"I can't take two solo acts
Simultaneously.
"We must have a contest
To see which has appeal."
"Oh we've got one of those!"
Said the two with a squeal.
So all of the fruit were formed up
In committee
To judge which was best,
Velvet-voiced, cute and witty.
They each sang a song,
The fruit gave each a score.
The applause was half-hearted,
In fact both were a bore.

The durian smiled and said:

"There, told you so.
"Now just to please me,
Have a go as a duo."
They apples reluctantly gave it a try
And after a Chorus or two had gone by
They began to enjoy singing in harmony
And they danced a duet just as neat as
could be.
The ovanges cheered,
the boy apples swooned
As Edwina and Agnes
Strutted and crooned.
And when the song ended,
The fruit all went wild.
Edwina and Agnes,
They bowed and they smiled.
"All right, we'll do it together," they said.
Durian Joe gave them pats on the head.

Edwina and Agnes became major stars.
They bought houses at Malibu Peach
And big cars.
They had money and fame
And sold millions of albums.
They had servants

Mostly Mexican girl plums.

So I tell you: of selfish ambition beware.
For two apples to make it, they must be ...

   a pear.

www.ingramcontent.com/pod-product-compliance
Lightning Source LLC
LaVergne TN
LVHW070538070526
838199LV00076B/6804